Yiayia Next Door

To our mother, Teresa, whose love and care for others inspired this book.

Mum, losing you has caused us unimaginable pain, despair, sorrow and heartache.

It has also created unexpected magic and connection, taking us by complete surprise.
Yiayia and the Yiayia Next Door community have collectively wrapped their arms
around us, opened their hearts and fed our stomachs and our souls, just like you
would have wished. As our community grows, your love and ethos of kindness
to all travels further, reaching those who need it most.

We know you'd cherish this collection of recipes as much as we do. It's our tribute to
all the devoted and loving mothers, especially those who have overcome adversity for
the little ones in their lives. May we know them, may we be them, may we raise them.
Let's forever support and adore them.

With thanks and love that never ends, from your two boys,

Luke and Daniel

Yiayia
next door

Daniel & Luke Mancuso (with Yiayia)

plum. Pan Macmillan Australia

Contents

Introduction 9
To our Yiayia Next Door community, old and new 17

~~~~~~~~~~~~~~~~~~~~~~~~~~~~~~

Proino
Breakfast 21

Artoskevasmata
Pastries 35

Soupes
Soups 53

Zimarika & Rizi
Pasta, Bread & Rice 67

Thalassina & Kreatika
Seafood & Meat 101

Salates & Lahanika
Salads & Vegetables 135

Glika
Sweets 169

~~~~~~~~~~~~~~~~~~~~~~~~~~~~~~

Thanks 201
Index 203

Introduction

by Tom Cowie, journalist, *The Age*

How well do you know your neighbours? For many of us, the extent of our relationship with the people we live next door to might constitute a bit of small talk while putting the bins out or collecting the mail during a holiday.

That's not to say we wouldn't like to be on better terms with those around us. It's just that, with our busy modern lives, we tend to stick with the people we know, and any thirst for a new connection can easily be satisfied by the endless possibilities offered by a phone screen.

Neighbourly friendship might be thought of as being a bit old fashioned but there are some people trying to keep it alive.

In a suburban street in Melbourne's north, two young men and their elderly neighbours have captured the hearts of people yearning to connect with the world around them.

For brothers Daniel and Luke Mancuso, their relationship with 'Yiayia' and 'Pappou' is a very special one indeed.

It is a bond built over generations between two families who have shared a fence for decades. Later, they were brought even closer by an unspeakable tragedy. The language that unites them is food, a dialect we can all understand.

I first met the famous 'Yiayia Next Door' in May 2019 after reaching out to Daniel and Luke through their Instagram account. I soon found out that there was a lot more to the story than what appeared on the surface.

What started off as a bit of fun posting videos of Yiayia sharing her cooking has become its own social movement, sparking important conversations about community and looking out for each other. It's even led to this cookbook that you are reading.

But to begin with, the whole thing was a bit of a mystery. I had the same question as many of their fans when I first watched Daniel and Luke's videos online: who are these guys?

The videos recorded by phone were often shot the same way. They showed several sets of hands reaching over an unassuming green and cream steel Colorbond fence to deliver and receive a platter, plate or dish.

While the characters themselves were off screen, the real star of the show was the food. It could be chicken and rice, or a warm pot of lentil soup. Whatever it was, Yiayia's home cooking looked so tasty you could almost smell it through the screen, once the foil or plastic wrap was peeled back.

'Thank you, Yiayia,' was how the brothers always responded, calling her 'grandmother' in Greek.

There were tens of thousands of people following the account, even before they knew anything about what had brought these neighbours together. Many commented that the relationship between Yiayia and the brothers reminded them of their own yiayia, or that they wished they lived next to someone like Yiayia.

Working as a newspaper journalist, my editor at the time asked me to check out how the relationship had started. I wasn't the first to wonder; other media outlets had already drawn attention to the account as a viral online curiosity, including morning television shows, pop culture websites and Greek newspaper *Neos Kosmos*.

The premise of the coverage was that these two men had hit the jackpot by moving into a share house located next door to a very hospitable neighbour. Proud Greeks said the yiayia was displaying perfect *philoxenia*, literally translating to 'friendship to a stranger'.

But while it may have looked like it, the people involved weren't really strangers.

'There's a bit more to this that we'd like to share,' Daniel told me when I reached out to him.

I had a feeling that might be the case. In preparation for an interview, I had found several news stories about a shocking case of family violence that had taken place in the same house several years earlier.

When I visited to record an interview, Daniel and Luke told me what unfolded one night in 2013, and in the years since.

As a welcomed guest, Yiayia's hospitality was extended to me as soon as I got there. I walked through her bountiful veggie garden, commenting on the flourishing lemon tree and strings of dried chillies hanging from the roof. She gave me bags full of both to take home later.

The Age's photographer, Joe Armao, took Yiayia's photo, however she refused to have her face included in the frame. 'Not the face!' she said repeatedly, preferring to remain anonymous and allow the brothers to be the centre of attention. She didn't really see what the fuss was about.

Inside, there was a plate of spanakopita – flaky pastry stuffed with salty spinach and cheese – to eat with our morning coffee, as I heard more about this remarkable story.

In 2013, Teresa Mancuso – after the breakdown of her marriage – was living with her own mother, while her sons lived with their father. Teresa had grown up in her parents' brick house in Melbourne's northern suburbs with her three siblings, attending the nearby high school.

Yiayia and Pappou lived next door and had known the Mancusos for decades. The families were long-time neighbours in a part of Melbourne known for its large number of Italian and Greek clans, who had moved in during the wave of migration to Australia after World War II.

Daniel and Luke were relieved when their parents' marriage ended after 23 years in 2010 because it had been so volatile. But the break-up had only led to more aggression from their father.

On that night in July 2013, Teresa returned home from the family's regular Monday night dinner. Tragically, it was the last time her family would see her alive.

It was Yiayia next door who heard her cries for help and called the police, but it was too late.

Almost immediately, everyone in the family suspected the boys' father of the murder, despite very little evidence connecting him with the crime. It took nearly two years for police to charge him but he was eventually put on trial and found guilty.

~~~~~~~~~~

Teresa had always wanted Daniel and Luke to live with her at her childhood home until she found her own place to move into. That never happened while she was alive but they later made the difficult decision to move in as a way of honouring her memory.

They've since renovated the house, with freshly painted walls and shiny new floorboards. Some of the Italian–Australian touches from when it was first built have been retained, such as the 1970s-era tiles and the white pillars out the front. Once a crime scene, the garage has become a man cave where they hang out with friends, playing table tennis or darts. Daniel works as a graphic designer, while Luke is a barber.

After they moved in next door, Yiayia quickly took Daniel and Luke under her wing. She regularly sent food around to the house and they became family to her.

'She gets angry if we call her by name,' says Daniel. 'She'll respond with "what did you say?" and we'll reply "sorry, Yiayia".'

Yiayia has one grandchild in her family but she tells people she has three: 'Two big ones and a little one,' she says.

'It was a pretty quick transition because she knew how hard it was for us,' says Daniel.

'She was just trying to be like a mum for us, or a nonna or yiayia. She wanted to do what she thought was necessary and right and give back to our mum, because our mum had given her all the help in the world when she was here. She says "I loved your mum very much. She was my favourite".'

They share celebrations like Greek Easter – eating barbecued lamb or pork and playing tsougrisma with dyed red eggs. Luke's favourite dish of Yiayia's is chicken and rice (see page 108), while Daniel likes kourabiethes, the shortbread 'moon' biscuits dusted with icing sugar (see page 172). Every time Yiayia whips something up in the kitchen, she makes enough for the boys. 'I love to cook, whenever I do I cook extra,' she says.

Often, Daniel and Luke come home from work wondering what to have for dinner and they'll get a phone call from Yiayia or Pappou. It's in her genes, Yiayia says, to feed them. If anything, she thinks they're too skinny and could eat more.

'I love it. I don't know why, it's [being a] yiayia,' she says. 'And their pappou too, he likes them to eat. Him more than me I think.'

'It's the sharing factor, you know that she's thinking of us,' says Luke. 'It's not just the food, it's the gesture that comes with it. It's just out of the kindness of her heart.'

While Yiayia loves to cook for them, the boys like to help her out too. They are happy to drive to the local market to pick up groceries or fill up the petrol tank in Pappou's lawnmower. They also share different fruits and vegetables they've grown in the back garden. Yiayia even taught Luke the best way to grow tomatoes.

It's not a case of paying her back but Daniel and Luke know what Yiayia has done for them, on top of all the food they enjoy. She gave evidence at the trial about the night their mother was killed, putting aside her own fear to call the police, and do what she could for Teresa.

Among the many posts on the Yiayia Next Door Instagram page are photos of Teresa. In nearly every picture, she smiles broadly at the camera, particularly when her sons are standing alongside her.

When her marriage ended, Teresa had a new life in front of her. She had found a new relationship and was fulfilling a career goal working as a flight attendant with Tiger Airways. Her old workmates still send messages to Daniel and Luke through the Yiayia Next Door page telling them how proud their mum would have been of them. When she was injured at work, Teresa kept busy by finding roles as an extra on television shows such as *Neighbours* and *Packed to the Rafters*.

Wherever she went in life, she connected with people. She was empathetic to others and more than happy to cook up a meal for friends and family when they visited. Like Yiayia does for Daniel and Luke now.

'We could have done anything with our lives and she would have been proud,' says Luke. 'It was just the type of person she was. She would always say "you boys are my world". And I think that's why she stayed in the relationship as long as she did. Because she felt trapped. Especially being a stay-at-home mum, she was young, she probably didn't have the finances to go out on her own. But I think she just wanted to be close to us.'

When they first started Yiayia Next Door, Daniel and Luke had no idea how big it would become. After our interview was published in *The Age*, Daniel and Luke were floored by the attention they received. The story was

one of the most read on *The Age*'s website all year and won the Melbourne Press Club feature writing award.

There was something special about the story that people really identified with, and there was much admiration for how Yiayia and the boys had supported each other through terrible adversity. It also helped that food was at the centre of it all.

'I received so many messages or calls from people saying they were crying and that they felt like they were part of that story,' says Daniel.

Since then, Daniel and Luke have grabbed the opportunity with both hands to become advocates against family violence and raise money for charity. Both know there is a real shortage of young men who are willing to speak up on the subject. They have told their story on radio stations Nova, ABC Melbourne and Triple J, as well as through televised interviews with *The Project*, SBS and Channel Seven.

Their work has grown to include ambassador roles with the Carlton Football Club and the Australian Childhood Foundation. There have been offers from people wanting to return their kindness, too. Travel agent Flight Centre helped Yiayia fly back to Greece to visit her ill sister, while the Victorian governor Linda Dessau invited them all for a visit. Sometimes, people will just drop loads of groceries on their front steps as a gift for Yiayia.

Most of all, Daniel and Luke want their story to encourage people to connect with their neighbours. Focusing on the positives and having fun is the best way to achieve this, they believe, which is why they have decided to publish this cookbook.

They hope people get enjoyment out of making meals they themselves are lucky enough to eat on a regular basis, or maybe they'll even drop some around to their own neighbours. Daniel and Luke encourage it as an icebreaker to become closer friends.

'It has been big for us because we're living in this home. We didn't have Nonna in here, we didn't have Mum,' says Luke of what Yiayia's cooking has meant to them. 'That sense of warmth and gathering has changed our lives.'

To our Yiayia Next Door community, old and new

We are proud to present this collection of Yiayia's authentic Greek recipes, along with a number of treasured family recipes kindly shared with us by our Yiayia Next Door social media community, without whom this book wouldn't be possible.

If you're new to our community or just hearing about us for the first time, we welcome you and hope our story inspires you to be the change you want to see in this unpredictable thing we call life.

To our long-time Yiayia Next Door followers, we are so thankful for you. It is because of you that the idea of making a cookbook first came about. We were constantly receiving messages and comments, asking how to make Yiayia's famous chicken and rice or lentil soup. So we listened and thought, why not open up the opportunity to our community and let them fill the rest of the cookbook with recipes close to their hearts? We put out the call on social media, our community responded, and the result is the book you hold in your hands.

As well as filling up your tummies with nostalgia, we hope this recipe collection will show you just how powerful having a sense of community can be. After all, we don't heal in isolation, but in connection.

Without the kindness of our community and, of course, a very special lady next door, we would not have the power and hope to be everything our beautiful mother wanted us to be. Quite simply, happy and free.

Today we are living the lives our mother always wanted us to live.

Even though we lost our whole world when our mum was taken from us, the power that has come after her death has inspired so many people. We wish we could still share life's precious moments with her, but her light shines brighter than ever through what we have accidentally built with Yiayia Next Door. This is our mum's legacy, and it's ever so fitting because of the selfless soul she truly was and will always remain.

We will continue to be the best men we can be thanks to the guidance, love and devotion of our beautiful mother. Inspired by her compassion and kindness, with every purchase of this book we will donate a portion of the proceeds to the Australian Childhood Foundation, where we will continue to work to make children feel safe and help them recover from the trauma of abuse, violence and neglect.

We know the world can sometimes feel like a negative place, but its true power can be measured by good. While Yiayia's identity remains a mystery at her request, her actions are the definition of true selflessness and show how love really does generate love.

So, we encourage you to share these recipes with your community and to make every effort to provide the support and love your neighbour may very well be missing. You might already have your own Yiayia Next Door, or it could be you who becomes that helping hand over the fence!

It's now our turn to say what Yiayia always does as she passes one of her iconic home-cooked meals over the now equally iconic fence: 'We hope you like it!'

Daniel and Luke

Proino

Breakfast

Mizithra keftedes

Ricotta balls

Yiayia likes to make these ricotta balls for breakfast. As she likes to say, 'It's good to eat something different, not always eggs.'

SERVES 3–4

400 g fresh ricotta
½ teaspoon salt
handful of finely chopped
  flat-leaf parsley
1 egg, lightly beaten
2 tablespoons dried
  breadcrumbs
½ teaspoon dried oregano
80 ml (⅓ cup) canola oil

Gently squeeze the ricotta to remove any excess liquid. Place the ricotta in a bowl, add the salt, parsley, egg and breadcrumbs, then mix well to combine. Add the oregano and mix through, then roll the ricotta mixture into walnut-sized balls (you should get about 18 balls).

Heat the oil in a non-stick frying pan over high heat, add the ricotta balls and cook, repositioning them in the pan every 30 seconds or so to stop them sticking, for 2½–3 minutes, until all sides are golden brown.

Serve as they are and enjoy.

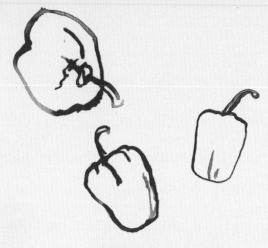

Tiganites piperies me htipita avga

Fried peppers with scrambled eggs

Yiayia uses home-grown peppers to make this scramble. The house fills with their beautiful aroma while cooking, which always brings a hungry Pappou into the kitchen. Yiayia and Pappou often enjoy this dish for breakfast, but you can also eat it for lunch.

SERVES 2–3

10 small mixed red, green and yellow bullhorn peppers (about 350 g) or sweet baby capsicums
80 ml (⅓ cup) canola oil
1 garlic clove, smashed
3 eggs, lightly beaten
½ teaspoon salt

To prepare the peppers or capsicums, push down on the stems, then immediately pull up to remove the cores in one piece. Slice the peppers or capsicums into thick rounds.

Heat the oil in a non-stick frying pan over medium–high heat. Add the pepper or capsicum rounds and garlic and cook for 5 minutes or until soft and lightly golden. Add the egg and salt and stir for 2 minutes or until the egg has scrambled.

Transfer to plates and serve immediately.

Fried egg,
Yiayia style

Add 3 tablespoons of canola oil
to a non-stick frying pan over
high heat. When hot, crack in
an egg and, using a spoon, start
scooping oil around and over
the egg for 1¼ minutes.

Htipito spanaki me avga

Scrambled eggs with spinach

Yiayia loves freshly picked spinach from her garden. In this recipe, she uses it to create her own twist on scrambled eggs. This is delicious on toast for breakfast or served as a side.

SERVES 3–4

1 bunch of English spinach (about 600 g)
2 tablespoons canola oil
2–3 eggs, lightly beaten
½ teaspoon salt

Trim any woody stems off the spinach, then wash the leaves thoroughly and drain. Using scissors, cut the spinach leaves into 2 cm wide strips. Transfer to a large saucepan and cover with cold water. Cover with a lid and bring to the boil over medium heat. Adjust the lid so it is slightly ajar and cook the spinach for 10 minutes. Drain and use a wooden spoon to squeeze out the excess liquid.

Heat the oil in a frying pan over medium heat, add the spinach and cook for 2 minutes. Add the egg and salt and stir for 2 minutes or until the egg has scrambled.

Serve while piping hot.

Scrambled eggs, Yiayia style

Crack two eggs into a bowl. Crumble 50 g of feta into the eggs and whisk with a fork, squishing the feta pieces down. Heat 20 g of unsalted butter in a non-stick frying pan over low heat, then add the egg mixture and turn up the heat to high. Keep mixing with the fork until the eggs are cooked to your liking.

Artoskevasmata

Pastries

Spanakopita

Yiayia was a newlywed when a relative visited and showed her how to make spanakopita. She had never seen dough stretched and pulled so thinly! The first time she made it, it was a big success, which made Yiayia's new in-laws very proud.

SERVES 12

1 bunch of English spinach (about 600 g), washed and roughly chopped
1 tablespoon olive oil
1 small onion, chopped
250 g feta, crumbled
2 eggs, lightly beaten
salt and black pepper

Spanakopita dough

5 g fresh yeast (see Note page 178) or ½ teaspoon instant dried yeast
400 ml warm water, plus extra if needed
600 g (4 cups) special white flour or 00 flour, plus extra for dusting
1 tablespoon salt
3 tablespoons olive oil, plus extra for brushing
125 g unsalted butter

To make the spanakopita dough, mix the yeast with a little of the warm water and set aside for a few minutes, until starting to bubble slightly.

Combine the flour and salt in a large bowl and make a well in the centre. Add the yeast mixture and remaining warm water, then use your hands to form a rough dough – it should be soft and a little sticky. Add a little more warm water if needed.

Turn the dough out onto a lightly floured work surface and knead for about 5 minutes, until the dough no longer sticks to your hands. The dough should be soft, smooth and pliable. Divide into six balls.

Working with one ball at a time, use your hand to flatten the dough balls into 1 cm thick discs. Brush each dough disc with a little olive oil, then line them up next to each other, cover with plastic wrap and set aside for 45–60 minutes to rest.

Meanwhile, heat a large saucepan over medium heat. Add the spinach and cook for 3–4 minutes, until wilted. Transfer to a colander and use the back of a spoon to press out the excess liquid. Set aside to cool slightly.

Heat the oil in a frying pan over medium heat, add the onion and cook for about 5 minutes, until translucent. Set aside to cool.

Combine the spinach, onion, feta, egg and salt and pepper to taste in a large bowl. Set aside.

For the dough, heat the oil and butter in a small saucepan until the butter melts, then remove from the heat and set aside.

Preheat the oven to 200°C (180°C fan-forced).

Brush the base and side of a 38 cm round shallow baking dish with olive oil.

Prepare a work surface by placing a large clean cloth or plastic tablecloth on a table and, if using a plastic tablecloth, sticking the edges to the table with sticky tape (this will prevent the tablecloth from bunching when you stretch the dough). Working with one disc of dough at a time, place the dough on the cloth and use your hands to gently stretch it as thinly as possible, until it is large enough to overhang the dish (see page 44, top right image). Tear off any thick bits of dough at the edges. Transfer one dough sheet to the prepared dish, allowing the excess dough to hang over the side of the dish. Brush the sheet all over with the melted butter and oil mixture. Repeat with another two sheets of dough and melted butter and oil mixture, then spread the filling evenly over the dough. Top the filling with the remaining dough sheets, brushing with the butter and oil mixture between each layer.

Fold the overhanging dough over the top of the pie, gently stretching it across the top as far as it will go, then brush all over with the remaining butter and oil mixture. Transfer to the oven and bake for 40–50 minutes, until golden brown.

Cut into slices and serve warm.

Spanakopita, see page 38

Strifti pita

Cheese pie

When Yiayia went to visit her sister in Greece a couple of years ago, she made strifti pita at her cousin's house. The oven was in use, so Yiayia walked to the local bakery and asked them to cook the pie for her. On her way back to the house, people stopped her and asked if they could try some. Being friendly, Yiayia gave out so many pieces that when she finally arrived home most of it had been eaten. The moral of the story is that you should always make two pies.

SERVES 4–6

3 tablespoons canola oil, plus extra for brushing
125 g unsalted butter
1 x quantity spanakopita dough (see page 38)
330 g Bulgarian sheep's feta, crumbled

Heat the oil and butter in a small saucepan until the butter melts, then remove from the heat and set aside.

Divide the spanakopita dough into four balls. Lightly flatten each ball into a disc and brush with a little of the butter and oil mixture.

Prepare a work surface by placing a large clean cloth or plastic tablecloth on a table and, if using a plastic tablecloth, sticking the edges to the table with sticky tape (this will prevent the tablecloth from bunching when you stretch the dough). Working with one disc of dough at a time, place the dough on the cloth and use your hands to gently stretch it as thinly as possible (see page 44, top right image), until it is roughly 80 cm × 80 cm. Tear off any thick bits of dough at the edges.

Using a tablespoon or pastry brush, streak some of the butter and oil mixture across the dough, then scatter over a little of the feta.

Using the tablecloth to assist you, lift one side of the dough sheet and roll the dough into a long sausage shape, stopping at the halfway point. Do the same on the opposite side. It should look like two long sausages sitting side by side (see pages 44–45 for step-by-step images).

Preheat the oven to 180°C (160°C fan-forced).

Roll the two dough sausages around each other to form a coil, then transfer to the centre of a greased dish. Repeat with the remaining dough, butter and oil mixture and feta, coiling each double strand of dough sausages around the previous one until you have filled the dish with one large coil. Transfer to the oven and bake for about 30 minutes, rotating the dish halfway through cooking, until the pastry is a light golden brown.

Cut into slices and serve.

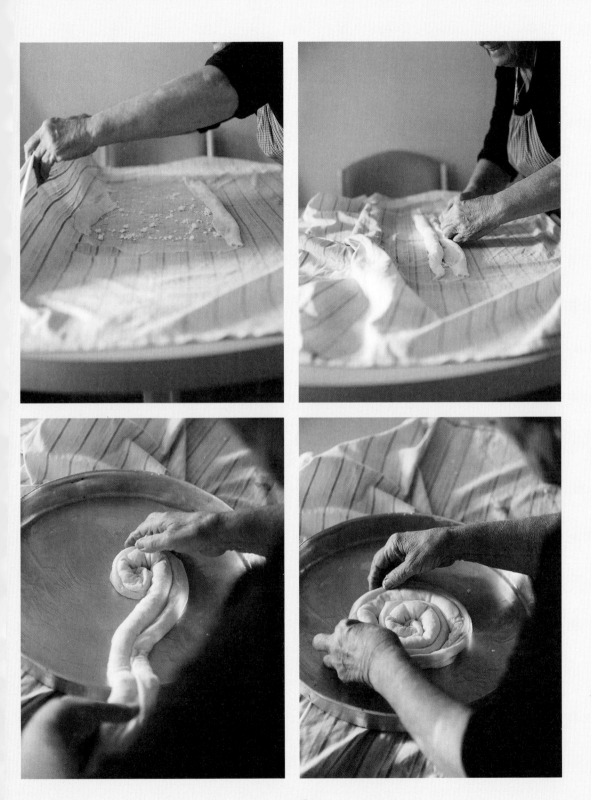

Kreatopita me praso

Mince & leek filo pie

Tired of making the traditional spinach filling for this Macedonian pie, Yiayia decided to try something different using mince and leek. Unsurprisingly, it was another hit with the family.

SERVES 12

1 x quantity spanakopita dough (see page 38)
3 tablespoons olive oil, plus extra for brushing
80 ml (⅓ cup) canola oil
1 leek, white and pale green part only, diced
1 large onion, diced
360 g mince (half beef topside, half pork fillet, minced twice; ask your butcher to do this for you)
2 teaspoons salt
125 g unsalted butter

Divide the spanakopita dough into six balls. Working with one ball at a time, use your hand to flatten the dough into 1 cm thick discs.

Brush each dough disc with a little olive oil, then line all the discs up next to each other, cover with plastic wrap and set aside for 45–60 minutes to rest.

Meanwhile, heat 2 tablespoons of the canola oil in a frying pan over medium heat, add the leek and onion and cook for about 6 minutes, until soft and translucent. Add the remaining canola oil and increase the heat to medium–high. Add the mince and salt and cook, breaking up any lumps with the back of a wooden spoon, for 5–6 minutes, until well browned. Remove from the heat and set aside to cool.

Heat the olive oil and butter in a small saucepan until the butter melts, then remove from the heat and set aside.

Preheat the oven to 200°C (180°C fan-forced). Lightly grease a 38 cm round shallow baking dish.

Prepare a work surface by placing a large clean cloth or plastic tablecloth on a table and, if using a plastic tablecloth, sticking the edges to the table with sticky tape (this will prevent the tablecloth from bunching when you stretch the dough). Working with one disc of dough at a time, place the dough on the cloth and use your hands to gently stretch it as thinly as possible (see page 44, top right image), until it is large enough to overhang the dish. Tear off any thick bits of dough at the edges. Transfer one dough sheet to the prepared dish, allowing the excess dough to hang over the side of the dish. Brush the sheet all over with the melted butter and oil mixture. Repeat with another two sheets of dough and melted butter and oil mixture, then spread the mince and leek filling evenly over the dough. Top the filling with the remaining dough sheets, brushing with the butter and oil mixture between each layer.

Fold the overhanging dough over the top of the pie, gently stretching it across the top as far as it will go, then brush all over with the remaining butter and oil mixture. Transfer to the oven and bake for 40–50 minutes, until golden brown. Cut into slices and serve warm.

Tiropita tis Yiayia

Yiayia's egg & feta filo pie

Inspired by a spinach shortage, Yiayia decided to make a pie using just egg and feta.
It was a great success, so Yiayia started to make it regularly and a new favourite was born.
Although the ingredients are simple, it is absolutely delicious and very filling.

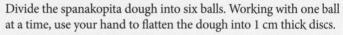

SERVES 12

1 x quantity spanakopita dough
(see page 38)
3 tablespoons olive oil, plus
extra for brushing
125 g unsalted butter
3 eggs, lightly beaten
330 g Bulgarian feta, crumbled

Divide the spanakopita dough into six balls. Working with one ball at a time, use your hand to flatten the dough into 1 cm thick discs.

Brush each dough disc with a little olive oil, then line all the discs up next to each other, cover with plastic wrap and set aside for 45–60 minutes to rest.

Heat the olive oil and butter in a small saucepan until the butter melts, then remove from the heat and set aside.

Preheat the oven to 200°C (180°C fan-forced). Lightly grease a 38 cm round shallow baking dish.

Using a fork, whisk together the egg and feta in a large bowl. Use the fork to press down and mash any large pieces of feta.

Prepare a work surface by placing a large clean cloth or plastic tablecloth on a table and, if using a plastic tablecloth, sticking the edges to the table with sticky tape (this will prevent the tablecloth from bunching when you stretch the dough). Working with one disc of dough at a time, place the dough on the cloth and use your hands to gently stretch it as thinly as possible (see page 44, top right image), until it is large enough to overhang the dish. Tear off any thick bits of dough at the edges. Transfer one dough sheet to the prepared dish, allowing the excess dough to hang over the side of the dish. Brush the sheet all over with the melted butter and oil mixture. Repeat with another two sheets of dough and melted butter and oil mixture, then spoon the egg and feta filling evenly over the dough. Top the filling with the remaining dough sheets, brushing with the butter and oil mixture between each layer.

Fold the overhanging dough over the top of the pie, gently stretching it across the top as far as it will go, then brush all over with the remaining butter and oil mixture. Transfer to the oven and bake for 40–50 minutes, until golden brown. Cut into slices and serve warm.

Debbie Xanthopoulos,
Victoria

Tiropita

Filo cheese pie

Greeks love their pies. They are a food that gives us a homely feeling. Growing up in a Greek home, pies were considered a unique specialty made by the matriarch of the family. Aside from being delicious, you could always grab a slice whenever you were hungry.

Think of spanakopita, manitaropita or sfakianopita and they all have one thing in common: cheese! But out of all the Greek pies, tiropita – or pita for short – is my favourite, and I promise that this pie will amaze your friends and family with its crisp and tangy flavour. A mature feta gives the pie a bold and salty flavour, so be careful with how much salt you add in the seasoning.

SERVES 4–6

200 g fresh firm ricotta
200 g mature feta, crumbled
300 g (2 cups) special white flour or 00 flour, plus extra for dusting
pinch of salt
2 tablespoons white wine vinegar
90 ml olive oil
60 g unsalted butter

Place the ricotta and feta in a large bowl and use a wooden spoon to mix them together until well combined.

Combine the flour, salt, vinegar, 3 tablespoons of the olive oil and 125 ml (½ cup) of water in a large bowl and mix to form a rough dough. Transfer to a lightly floured work surface and knead for about 5 minutes, until smooth and elastic.

Melt the butter in a saucepan over low heat, add the remaining oil, then remove from the heat.

Divide the dough in half and roll out each half into a 2 cm thick disc. Brush with some of the butter and oil mixture, then cover the discs with plastic wrap and aside to rest for 30 minutes.

Preheat the oven to 200°C (180°C fan-forced). Brush a little of the butter and oil mixture over a large baking tray.

Prepare a work surface by placing a large clean cloth or plastic tablecloth on a table and, if using a plastic tablecloth, sticking the edges to the table with sticky tape (this will prevent the tablecloth from bunching when you stretch the dough). Working with one disc of dough at a time, place the dough on the cloth and use your hands to gently stretch it as thinly as possible (see opposite), until it is roughly 80 cm × 80 cm.

Lightly brush the dough with some of the butter and oil mixture, then use a spoon or your hand to gently smear half the feta mixture over the stretched dough. Remove the sticky tape (if using) from the tablecloth, then start rolling the dough sheet by lifting the edge of the tablecloth closest to you and letting the dough roll over itself to enclose the filling and to form a long sausage. Roll the sausage into itself to form a coil, then repeat with the remaining dough, a little more of the butter and oil mixture and the remaining feta mixture to make another long sausage. Wrap the sausage around the first coil to make a large snail shape. Brush the remaining butter and oil mixture over the top.

Transfer to the prepared tray and bake for about 35 minutes, until golden, then slice and serve. See overleaf for the finished tiropita.

Tiropita (filo cheese pie), see page 48

Soupes

Soups

Fasolada (bean soup), see page 56

Fasolada

Bean soup

Fasolada is a Friday-night staple in Yiayia's house. For religious reasons, Yiayia abstains from eating meat or dairy on a Friday, so she always makes a pot of bean soup or lentil soup (see page 58) to eat instead.

SERVES 6

600 g (3 cups) dried lima beans or other white beans, soaked in cold water overnight
1 small onion, finely chopped
1 red bullhorn pepper (or capsicum), finely chopped
½ leek, white and pale green part only, finely chopped
80 ml (⅓ cup) olive oil
1 tablespoon ground paprika
1 tablespoon salt
1 bunch of flat-leaf parsley, finely chopped
2 litres boiling water, plus extra if needed
crusty bread, to serve
black olives, to serve

Drain the beans and place them in a large saucepan. Add the remaining ingredients, except the bread and olives, and bring to the boil over high heat, stirring occasionally. Reduce the heat to medium–low and cook, covered, for about 30 minutes, until the beans are tender and cooked through, adding extra boiling water if needed. The soup should be thick and hearty.

Divide the soup among bowls and serve with crusty bread and black olives on the side.

Fakes

Lentil soup

Another Friday-night staple, Yiayia promises this hearty soup will warm up your insides and put a smile on your face.

SERVES 6

200 g (1 cup) dried brown lentils, rinsed
2.25 litres boiling water
3 tablespoons olive oil
1 onion, finely chopped
1 small red bullhorn pepper (or capsicum), finely chopped
1 small green bullhorn pepper (or capsicum), finely chopped
2 garlic cloves, finely chopped
1½ teaspoons ground paprika
1 teaspoon salt
large handful of chopped flat-leaf parsley

Check the lentils for any stones or shrivelled pieces and discard.

Place the lentils in a large saucepan and add enough cold water to just cover them. Bring to the boil over medium–high heat and cook for 10 minutes. Drain well, then return the lentils to the pan and add the boiling water. Bring to the boil, then reduce the heat to medium, cover with a lid and simmer for 35 minutes or until the lentils are tender.

Meanwhile, heat the oil in a frying pan over medium–high heat. Add the onion, peppers and garlic and cook for 7 minutes or until soft. Add the paprika and cook for about 1 minute, until fragrant, then stir the mixture through the cooked lentils, add the salt and simmer for 5 minutes.

Divide the soup among bowls, sprinkle over some chopped parsley and serve.

Tania Gogos Wilson,
Victoria

Eftichia's avgolemono

I was obsessed with avgolemono soup when I was a child. My yiayia Eftichia and thea (aunty) Angela would always have a pot bubbling away for me on their hotplates whenever I visited either of them. We spent every weekend at my yiayia's house while my parents attended to their social commitments (usually with a Greek nightclub thrown in, which were great back in the day in Melbourne). I would try and set a record of how many bowls of avgolemono I could eat in a day, and my yiayia would send me home with a big Greek coffee jar full of soup so I could enjoy it throughout the week.

My yiayia was an extraordinary woman who died at the age of 99. Her son (my dad) was Demetrious Gogos, the founder of Melbourne's Greek newspaper *Neos Kosmos*, and many stories were written in the paper about my yiayia's life. She was very famous for her sweets.

SERVES 6–8

salt and black pepper
1.3 kg whole chicken
6 spring onions, 2 roughly chopped, 4 sliced
5 celery stalks, strings removed, 1 chopped into large chunks, 4 sliced
½ bunch of dill, roughly chopped, plus extra to serve (optional)
170 ml (⅔ cup) olive oil, preferably Greek
150 g (¾ cup) medium-grain rice
2 eggs
80 ml (⅓ cup) freshly squeezed lemon juice

Fill a large saucepan with 5.25 litres of water and season with 1 tablespoon of salt. Bring to the boil over high heat.

Meanwhile, smother the chicken with 1 tablespoon each of salt and pepper and stuff the roughly chopped spring onion, celery chunks and half the dill inside the cavity. Gently lower the chicken into the boiling water and add the olive oil and remaining spring onion, celery and dill. Reduce the heat to a simmer and cook the chicken for about 1 hour, until tender.

Remove the chicken from the pan and set aside, then add the rice to the simmering water and cook for 20 minutes or until cooked through.

When cool enough to handle, gently remove the meat from the chicken carcass and shred into bite-sized pieces. You can either add the chicken to the soup at the end of cooking or serve it on the side.

In a large bowl, whisk the eggs with electric beaters, then gradually pour in the lemon juice, whisking as you go. Add six or seven ladles of the soup stock and continue to whisk until light and fluffy, then pour the lemon–egg mixture into the soup stock, stirring constantly for 1–2 minutes. Return the chicken to the soup, if you like, and gently heat through.

Divide the soup among bowls and serve scattered with extra dill (if desired) and some freshly ground black pepper.

Nicholas Giakoumelos,
New South Wales

Giakoumelos family's avgolemono

This is my favourite winter-warming soup from my mum's recipe collection. It's easy to make and very delicious. I always make a large pot to feed my three teenage, soon-to-be adult, children. They love it.

SERVES 6–8

2 tablespoons olive oil
2 onions, finely chopped
4 garlic cloves, roughly chopped
1.3 kg whole chicken
2 carrots, diced
3–4 celery stalks, diced
220 g (1 cup) arborio rice
2 eggs, at room temperature, separated
juice of 2 lemons
salt and black pepper

Heat the olive oil in a large stockpot over medium heat. Add the onion and garlic and cook for 5 minutes or until the onion is soft and translucent. Add the chicken and enough water to completely cover the meat, then increase the heat to medium–high and bring to the boil. Reduce the heat to a simmer and cook for 1 hour, adding more water if necessary to ensure that the chicken remains completely submerged.

Using tongs, remove the chicken and set aside to cool. Add the carrot, celery and rice to the pot and simmer for 25–30 minutes, until the rice is soft. Remove from the heat.

Whisk the egg whites until fluffy, then, whisking constantly, slowly add the egg yolks, lemon juice and 250 ml (1 cup) of liquid from the pot. Whisk until well combined and glossy.

Shred the chicken, then add to the pot. Stir through the egg mixture, then warm through over low heat for 1–2 minutes. Season with salt and pepper to taste, then divide among bowls and serve.

Fithosoupa

Chicken noodle soup

When Yiayia's grandson, Tex, visits his grandparents his first request is always, 'Chicken soup, Yiayia, chicken soup!' It's his favourite dish and he never gets bored of it. It's simple and nourishing.

SERVES 4

9 chicken drumsticks
1 teaspoon salt
1 cup (about 2 nests) broken-up fide pasta (very fine, long Greek noodles sold in nests; substitute broken-up angel hair pasta if necessary)
1 egg, lightly beaten

Place the chicken drumsticks in a stockpot and cover with plenty of cold water. Bring to the boil, covered, over high heat, then skim off any foam that has risen to the surface. Reduce the heat to medium, place the lid slightly ajar and simmer for 50 minutes.

Remove the pot from the heat. Remove the chicken drumsticks and set aside until cool enough to handle, then, using your hands, pull the meat off five of the drumsticks and shred. Save the remaining drumsticks for another use.

Return the chicken stock to medium heat, add the salt and fide noodles and stir. Add the shredded chicken and cook for 2 minutes or until the chicken is heated through and the noodles are cooked. Remove from the heat and allow to cool a little, then stir through the beaten egg.

Divide the chicken noodle soup among bowls and serve.

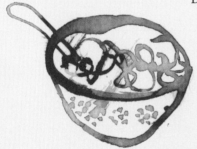

Connie Siopoulos,
South Australia

Giouvarlakia

Meatball soup

This dish brings back childhood memories of my mum, who would often make this meatball soup during winter. When I first travelled to Greece to visit my yiayia, I discovered that she also made giouvarlakia, and I fondly remember helping her roll the meatballs. This soup brings me so much comfort and wonderful memories of the two strong women in my life.

Serves 6–8

80 ml (⅓ cup) extra-virgin
   olive oil
1 leek, white and pale green
   part only, finely sliced
1 potato, peeled and diced
1 chicken or vegetable
   concentrated stock pot
   (or use 500 ml/2 cups chicken
   or vegetable stock)
⅓ cup chopped flat-leaf parsley
3 eggs, separated
juice of 2 lemons

Meatballs

1 kg beef mince
2 eggs
1 large onion, grated
100 g (½ cup) long-grain rice
3 tablespoons chopped
   dill fronds
1 tablespoon chopped
   mint leaves
½ cup chopped flat-leaf parsley
salt and black pepper

To make the meatballs, place the ingredients in a large bowl and, using your hands, mix until well combined. Roll the mixture into meatballs a little smaller than a golf ball and set aside.

Heat the olive oil in a stockpot over medium heat, add the leek and potato and cook for about 5 minutes, until the leek is softened. Add 3 litres of water (or 2.5 litres if using liquid stock), along with the concentrated stock pot and bring to the boil. Carefully lower the meatballs into the stock, then reduce the heat to a simmer and cook for 30 minutes, skimming off any foam that rises to the surface. Stir through the parsley, then remove the pan from the heat.

Meanwhile, whisk the egg yolks and lemon juice until nice and creamy.

Whisk the egg whites until combined, then whisk in the egg yolk mixture. Whisking quickly and constantly, add two ladles of the soup stock, incorporating each fully before adding the next. Pour the egg mixture into the pot and stir gently to avoid breaking up the meatballs.

Divide the soup and meatballs among bowls and serve.

Zimarika & Rizi

Pasta, Bread & Rice

Psomi spitíko

Homemade bread

Yiayia still uses the original dish she brought with her from Greece to Australia to make this simple bread. It was a gift from her mother, who packed it in Yiayia's suitcase among her clothing.

Makes 3 small loaves

30 g fresh yeast (see Note
  page 178) or 3 teaspoons
  instant dried yeast
900 g special white flour or
  00 flour, plus extra for
  dusting and kneading
1 teaspoon canola oil
¾ teaspoon salt

Fill a kettle with water, bring to the boil, then allow the water to cool to lukewarm. Place the yeast in a jug, add 80 ml (⅓ cup) of the lukewarm water and stir until dissolved.

Sift the flour into a large bowl and make a well in the centre. Add the yeast mixture, oil and salt, then gradually add 500 ml (2 cups) of the lukewarm water, while mixing together with your other hand. Continue to mix until well combined, then transfer the dough to a well-floured work surface.

Knead for about 10 minutes, dusting with more flour as you go, until the dough is soft and bounces back when you press a finger into it. Roll the dough into a ball.

Lightly flour a bowl that's just larger than the dough ball, then add the dough, cover with a clean tea towel and tuck in the sides. Wrap the entire bowl in another tea towel or small towel to keep warm, then set aside in a warm place for about 50 minutes, until the dough has risen to the top of the bowl.

Preheat the oven to 200°C (180°C fan-forced). Lightly flour a large baking tray with low sides.

Dust your work surface again with flour, then turn out the dough and knead for 5 minutes or until bubbles appear on the surface. Tear the dough into three pieces, then lightly knead each piece and roll into balls using well-floured hands.

If you have a patterned embossing tool, lightly press it into the top of the dough balls, then prick each ball with a toothpick at the top, bottom, left and right, then once in the centre. Transfer the dough to the prepared tray with space between each ball of dough. Cover with a tea towel and set aside for 10 minutes, then transfer to the oven and cook, rotating the tray occasionally, for 25–30 minutes or until the bread is lightly golden and there is a hollow sound when it's tapped on the bottom.

Allow to cool slightly and serve.

Elle Nikolaou-Abdo,
Victoria

Tiganopsomo me feta

Fried bread with feta

My Yiayia, Helen, who I am also named after, has made this fried bread recipe since before I can remember. She would make up to 15 loaves of bread each week, not only for her family to enjoy but everyone she met. With the leftover dough, she would make fried bread with feta (occasionally sprinkled with honey on top). People were constantly in awe of her talents and immense kindness. Food was her way of showing gratitude and love to the people around her, especially her family.

Growing up, I was blessed enough to live next door to my yiayia and pappou. We even shared a door through our backyards! I am so grateful I was able to spend so much time with Yiayia (and Pappou, of course), learning and consolidating the Greek language, listening to stories about their ancestors and upbringing, and discovering the traditional recipes that stayed with them for generations. Now, in 2021, after suffering two strokes in 2016 and 2018, and having to learn how to walk, talk and eat on her own again, I am a thousand times more grateful for the memories I have and the recipes she taught me. This fried bread recipe was the simplest of things, but always had a sense of family and community to it.

Makes 2

280 g plain flour, plus extra
   if needed and for dusting
1 teaspoon salt
1 teaspoon sugar
7 g sachet instant dried yeast
120 g Greek yoghurt
80 ml (⅓ cup) warm water,
   plus extra if needed
200 g feta, crumbled
125 ml (½ cup) olive oil
honey, to serve (optional)

Combine the flour, salt, sugar and yeast in a large bowl. Add the yoghurt and stir to combine, then gradually add the warm water and mix until it forms a dough. Knead in the bowl for about 5 minutes, until you have a light, non-sticky dough, adding a little more flour or water if necessary to achieve the right consistency.

Grease a large clean bowl with olive oil, then add the dough and cover with plastic wrap. Set aside in a warm place for 50 minutes or until doubled in size (covering the bowl with thick blankets or towels will create an airtight warm space for the dough to rise).

Poke a finger into the middle of the dough to deflate it, then transfer to a lightly floured work surface and knead for 1 minute. Divide the dough into quarters. Using a floured rolling pin, roll out the dough into four 20 cm discs, about 5 mm thick. Scatter the feta over two of the dough discs, leaving a 1 cm border. Top with the remaining dough discs and press and fold the edges, pinching inwards, to seal.

Heat half the olive oil in a large frying pan over medium heat. Add one of the stuffed dough discs and cook for 1 minute each side or until golden brown and cooked through. Transfer to a plate and repeat with the remaining oil and stuffed dough.

Serve hot or, for a sweet and salty twist, serve with a drizzle of honey on top.

Tsoureki tis Anne

Anne's Greek Easter bread

Yiayia's dear friend Anne spent the day with her to share and write down her tsoureki recipe, as Yiayia thinks Anne's Easter bread is nicer than her own. Anne was very happy to give her beloved recipe to Yiayia – a sign of true friendship!

~~~~~~

MAKES 4 SMALL LOAVES

60 g unsalted butter
3 tablespoons canola oil
4 eggs
3 teaspoons vanilla sugar
2 teaspoons ground pure
    mahlepi (a fruity Greek spice
    made from the inner kernels
    of Persian cherry stones;
    available from specialist
    Greek suppliers)
⅛ teaspoon ground nutmeg
⅛ teaspoon ground cloves
3 teaspoons orange zest
2 teaspoons lemon zest
250 g caster sugar
¼ teaspoon salt
125 ml (½ cup) warm water
65 g fresh yeast
850 g special white flour or
    00 flour, plus extra for dusting
2 tablespoons instant dried yeast
125 ml (½ cup) full-cream milk
3 tablespoons freshly squeezed
    orange juice
1½ tablespoons sesame seeds

Melt the butter in a small saucepan over low heat. Add the canola oil and stir it through, then remove from the heat.

Whisk three of the eggs in a large bowl, then add the vanilla sugar, mahlepi, nutmeg, clove and citrus zests and briefly whisk together. Add the sugar and salt and whisk until the ingredients are well combined.

Place the warm water in a large saucepan, crumble in the fresh yeast and stir until smooth. Add 50 g (⅓ cup) of the flour, along with the dried yeast and whisk to combine. Half-fill a sink with warm water, then add the pan, cover with a lid and leave to activate for 10–15 minutes.

Meanwhile, place the milk in a saucepan and briefly warm over low heat for about 1 minute. Stir in the orange juice, then pour the orange milk into the egg mixture, along with the butter and oil mixture and two-thirds of the remaining flour. Mix with a wooden spoon for 1 minute, until completely combined.

Add the activated yeast mixture and the remaining flour to the bowl and mix well until you have a thick dough. Transfer the dough to a lightly floured work surface and knead for about 5 minutes, until the dough bounces back when you press a finger into it.

Transfer the dough to a large clean bowl, then place in a reusable plastic bag and set aside in a warm spot for 2–3 hours, until at least doubled in size.

Lightly grease a large baking tray and line with baking paper.

When the dough has risen, lightly punch the surface to let the air out, then transfer to a lightly oiled work surface. Divide the dough into four equal portions. Working with one portion at a time, divide the dough into three even pieces. Roll each piece of dough into a rope about 2 cm thick. Press the ends together, then plait the three ropes together (see pages 80–81). Repeat the process with the remaining portions of dough.

Transfer the plaits to the prepared baking tray, about 10 cm apart, then cover with a clean tea towel and set aside to rise slightly for 1½–2 hours.

Preheat the oven to 200°C (180°C fan-forced).

Whisk the remaining egg with a splash of water and glaze the plaits. Sprinkle the sesame seeds on top, then place in the oven and bake for 20–25 minutes, until golden brown (see finished tsoureki pictured overleaf).

Tsoureki (Greek Easter bread), see pages 74 and 78

Debbie Xanthopoulos,
Victoria

Tsoureki tis Debbie

Debbie's Greek Easter bread

This recipe has been handed down through the generations in my family and I am honoured to share it with you. My grandparents migrated from Northern Greece to Australia in the 1960s, leaving behind my mother to look after her grandmother. She, and the local ladies in the village, taught my mother many traditional recipes including this Easter bread. As a result, my mother became an amazing cook and I am so grateful to her for sharing her tasty food with us.

Makes 2

125 ml (½ cup) warm water
15 g instant dried yeast
110 g (½ cup) sugar
600 g (4 cups) plain flour
¼ teaspoon mastiha chios (mastic)
3 large eggs
1½ teaspoons finely grated orange zest
80 ml (⅓ cup) freshly squeezed orange juice
1½ tablespoons sunflower oil
3 tablespoons full-cream milk
1½ teaspoons ground pure mahlepi (a fruity Greek spice made from the inner kernels of Persian cherry stones; available from specialist Greek suppliers)
½ teaspoon vanilla powder
pinch of salt
1 teaspoon bread improver
60 g unsalted butter, softened

Place the warm water, yeast, a pinch of the sugar and 2 tablespoons of the flour in a large bowl and stir to combine. Cover with plastic wrap and set aside for about 30 minutes, until bubbling.

Using a mortar and pestle, finely grind the mastiha chios, then immediately (see Note) transfer to a large bowl and add the remaining sugar, two of the eggs, the orange zest and juice, sunflower oil, milk, mahlepi, vanilla powder, salt and bread improver. Mix well, then add the activated yeast mixture and gradually add the remaining flour, mixing with your other hand to form a rough dough. Keeping the dough in the bowl, gradually add the softened butter, kneading as you go. Continue to knead for about 5 minutes, until the dough is soft and pliable.

Cover the bowl with plastic wrap and set aside in a warm spot for 2–3 hours, until at least doubled in size. If it's a cool day, you can heat the oven to 30°C, then turn it off and place the bowl inside to keep warm.

Gently punch the dough to deflate it, then cut into two equal portions. Working with one portion at a time, divide the portion into three pieces (do not flour your work surface!), then roll one piece into a sausage shape. Hold the ends in your hands, then gently stretch and shake the dough into a 40 cm long rope. This technique helps to form the characteristic stringy texture of tsoureki. Repeat with the other two pieces of dough.

Place the three dough ropes vertically in front of you, then plait from the top (see pages 80–81). Transfer the braid to a baking tray lined with baking paper, then repeat with the remaining dough to make another braid. Cover the braids with a clean tea towel and set aside in a warm spot for 1–2 hours, until almost doubled in size.

Preheat the oven to 180°C (160°C fan-forced).

In a small bowl, whisk the remaining egg with 1 tablespoon of water. Brush the top of each tsoureki with the glaze, being careful not to deflate them. Transfer to the oven and bake for 30–35 minutes, until golden brown and fluffy (see finished tsoureki pictured on page 77).

Store at room temperature, wrapped in plastic wrap, for 5–7 days.

Note

It's important to transfer the mastiha chios from the mortar immediately after grinding or else it will harden and stick to the surface.

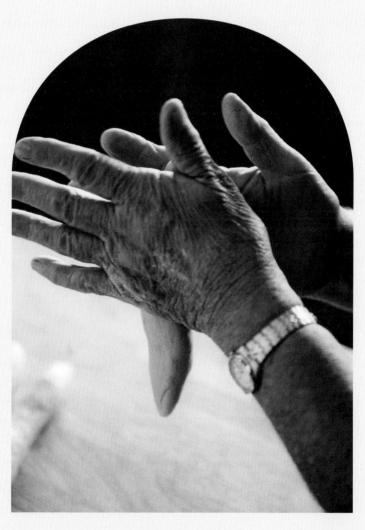

Kokkino rizi me kotopoulo & spanaki

Red rice with chicken & spinach

Yiayia's family love this dish and often ask her to make it for them. Yiayia is always happy to cook food for others. The paprika makes the rice a deep red colour, while the chilli flakes give the dish a hint of spice.

SERVES 4–6

8 chicken drumsticks
3 tablespoons olive oil
1 onion, diced
3 red bullhorn peppers
   (or capsicums), diced
1 teaspoon ground paprika
½ teaspoon chilli flakes
1 bunch of English spinach
   (about 600 g), washed
   and trimmed
500 g (2½ cups) medium-
   grain rice
1 teaspoon salt
crusty bread, to serve (optional)

Pour 2.5 litres of water into a large saucepan and bring to the boil over high heat. Reduce the heat to medium, add the chicken drumsticks and cook for 20 minutes, skimming off any foam that rises to the surface, until the meat starts to fall away from the bone. Using tongs, remove the chicken from the pan and set aside to cool. Keep the stock in the pan.

Meanwhile, heat the olive oil in a frying pan over medium heat, add the onion, pepper, paprika and chilli flakes and cook for about 5 minutes, until the vegetables are soft. Remove from the heat and set aside.

Using your hands, tear the spinach into even-sized pieces.

When cool enough to handle (not many people have hands as tough as Yiayia's), peel and discard the skin and fat from the chicken, then tear the meat into chunks. Discard the bones.

Bring the stock to the boil, then add the rice, the onion and pepper mixture, the chicken, spinach and salt. Stir until well combined, then reduce the heat to a simmer and cook for 15–20 minutes, until the rice is soft, but there is still some liquid remaining.

Divide the rice mixture among plates and serve with bread (if desired) to mop up the juices.

Kathy Marin,
Victoria

Spanakorizo

Spinach & rice

This is a village-style spanakorizo. There are so many variations, and this is one that my mum, Voula, made often. Spanakorizo tastes and smells like my childhood, and reminds me of all the warmth and love that Mum had to offer. When Mum became a yiayia herself, her grandchildren also enjoyed its deliciousness every bit as much as we did growing up. It is wholesome. It is Greek. It is memories on a plate.

SERVES 6–8

1 litre chicken or vegetable stock
125 ml (½ cup) extra-virgin olive oil
1 white onion, finely diced
2 garlic cloves, crushed
400 g can diced tomatoes or two large tomatoes, chopped
400 g (2 cups) medium-grain rice
400 g English or baby spinach, roughly chopped
salt and black pepper
250 ml (1 cup) boiling water, if needed
¼ cup chopped mint leaves
¼ cup chopped flat-leaf parsley
crumbled feta, to serve

Pour the stock into a saucepan and bring to a gentle boil.

Meanwhile, heat the olive oil in a large saucepan over low heat. Add the onion and cook for 5–7 minutes, until translucent, then add the garlic and cook for 1–2 minutes, until fragrant.

Add the tomatoes and stir for 1–2 minutes, then stir through the rice until coated in the tomato mixture. Add the hot stock and spinach and season with salt and pepper to taste, then gently cook, stirring frequently, for 15–20 minutes, until the rice is tender and most of the liquid is absorbed (gradually add some of the boiling water if the mixture starts to dry out, but you may not need it). Stir through the chopped herbs, then turn off the heat and allow the rice to sit for a few minutes.

Divide the spanakorizo among plates and serve with crumbled feta over the top.

Hílopites me keftedakia

Pasta squares with meatballs

Yiayia was fed up with cooking rice all the time, so one day she spiced things up by adding hilopites – Greek pasta squares – to this meatball dish instead. Everyone loved it. With one simple change, Yiayia had created a delicious new meal to share with family and friends.

SERVES 4

3 tablespoons canola oil
2 onions, finely chopped
350 g mince (half beef topside, half pork fillet, minced twice; ask your butcher to do this for you)
3 teaspoons salt
1 egg
handful of chopped flat-leaf parsley
3 tablespoons dried breadcrumbs
1 heaped teaspoon ground paprika
1 litre boiling water
250 g hilopites (Greek egg pasta squares)

Preheat the oven to 210°C (190°C fan-forced).

Heat the oil in a large frying pan over medium heat, add two-thirds of the onion and cook for 5 minutes or until soft and translucent. Increase the heat to medium–high, add half the mince and 1 teaspoon of the salt and cook, breaking up any lumps with the back of a wooden spoon, for 5 minutes or until well browned. Remove the pan from the heat and set aside.

Place the remaining mince and onion, the egg, parsley, breadcrumbs and 1 teaspoon of the remaining salt in a bowl and mix with your hands until well combined. Divide and shape the mixture into 12 small meatballs.

Spread the cooked mince mixture over the base of a 36 cm × 30 cm roasting tin or flameproof baking dish and place over medium heat. Sprinkle over the paprika and remaining salt, then pour in the boiling water. Sprinkle in the hilopites and stir well, then top with the meatballs. Carefully transfer the tin or dish to the oven and cook for 15 minutes. Give the mixture a stir, then cook for a further 5–10 minutes or until the hilopites and meatballs are cooked through.

Divide among plates and serve.

Yiayia's Kitchen Tips

Yiayia's generation was
reducing, reusing and recycling
long before it was a thing.
Here are her top tips for saving
money and minimising waste in
the kitchen, plus some general
cooking know-how.

1   Did you know you can reuse zip-lock bags and aluminium foil? Yiayia washes her used foil and bags, then hangs them out on the clothesline to dry. This is always a sign that good food is coming our way!

2   Save all those jars from the supermarket to use for your own homemade sauces and preserves. Sterilise them first by washing the jars and lids in hot, soapy water and rinsing well, or running them through a hot cycle in the dishwasher. Leave to air-dry on a clean tea towel, then you're good to go.

3   Who needs Tupperware? Save ice cream and butter containers to store leftovers in the fridge and freezer. The only downside is opening an ice cream container from Yiayia's freezer on a hot summer's day to find frozen soup or stew.

4   When preserving olives, Yiayia recommends putting the fruit in a bucket, filling it with cold water and adding a handful of salt. Leave it for two days, then replace the water (no need to add more salt) every two days for 10–14 days, depending on how bitter the olives are. When ready, give the olives a good rinse and place them in sterilised jars with salt, dried oregano and sliced garlic to taste.

5   Yiayia cooks all day every day, so always has a (recycled) container in the kitchen to collect food scraps for composting. Not only does this improve the soil in Yiayia and Pappou's garden, it is the single best way to reduce household waste.

6   Nothing is ever thrown away in Yiayia's household. All those rubber bands that come with fresh produce from the market are saved and reused in her pantry.

7   If you're lucky enough to have a kitchen outside (typically in the garage) or a barbecue, Yiayia recommends cooking any fish dishes out there to prevent the house from smelling.

8   When using a souvla rotisserie barbecue, always put a layer of sand underneath your coals to avoid burning a hole through the bottom.

9   If you've grown more chillies than you know what to do with, simply sew the stems together and hang them in a cool, dry spot indoors for about a week. Then you'll always have dried chillies on hand for cooking.

Lasagne

Our neighbourhood is full of love, support and sharing. Yiayia's dear late friend, Teresa Stoduto, lived across the street and taught her how to make this lasagne. Teresa was Italian and, like Yiayia, her English wasn't so good, but they understood the language of friendship and support. Teresa and Yiayia were friends for 40 years.

SERVES 10–12

80 ml (⅓ cup) canola oil
1 large onion, diced
500 g mince (half beef topside,
  half pork fillet, minced twice;
  ask your butcher to do this
  for you)
1.4 kg passata
½ teaspoon salt
½ teaspoon chilli flakes
1 teaspoon dried oregano
2 tablespoons chopped
  flat-leaf parsley
500 g dried lasagne sheets
500 g shredded mozzarella

Preheat the oven to 200°C (180°C fan-forced).

Heat 2 tablespoons of the oil in a large deep frying pan over medium–high heat, add the onion and cook for 5 minutes or until soft and translucent. Increase the heat to medium–high, add 2 tablespoons of the remaining oil and the mince and cook, breaking up any lumps with the back of a wooden spoon, for about 10 minutes, until well browned. Pour in the passata and stir through until well combined, then add the salt, chilli flakes, oregano and parsley and mix through. Remove the pan from the heat and set aside.

Meanwhile, bring a large saucepan of water to the boil.

Grease a 35 cm × 26 cm × 6.5 cm deep baking dish with the remaining oil and add a layer of the meat sauce. Working with one lasagne sheet at a time, blanch the pasta in the boiling water for 1 minute, then place on top of the meat sauce in a single layer. Sprinkle over some of the mozzarella. Repeat the layering of meat sauce, pasta and mozzarella until you have used all the ingredients, finishing with a layer of mozzarella. Cover the dish with foil, then transfer to the oven and cook for 25 minutes. Remove the foil and cook for a further 15 minutes or until golden.

Cut into portions and serve.

Pîlafî me kima

Baked rice with mince

Yiayia's mum taught her how to make this dish when she was only 15 years old. Yiayia calls her mum's dishes 'village food'. They were made using ingredients from the garden (or the neighbour's garden!) and the local surroundings. They are simple and comforting, and remind Yiayia of when she was a girl.

SERVES 3–4

3 tablespoons canola oil
1 large onion, diced
5 yellow bullhorn peppers
  (or capsicums), diced
220 g mince (half beef topside,
  half pork fillet, minced twice;
  ask your butcher to do this
  for you)
1 tablespoon salt
1 tablespoon ground paprika
2 teaspoons dried oregano
1 teaspoon chilli flakes
1 teaspoon black pepper
600 g medium-grain rice,
  well rinsed
1 litre boiling water
1 cup chopped flat-leaf parsley

Preheat the oven to 220°C (200°C fan-forced).

Heat the oil in a large frying pan over medium heat, add the onion and cook for about 5 minutes, until soft and translucent. Add the pepper and cook for 5 minutes or until soft, then increase the heat to medium–high and add the mince, salt, paprika, oregano, chilli flakes and pepper and cook, breaking up any lumps of mince with the back of a wooden spoon, for 5 minutes or until well browned. Remove from the heat and stir through the rice.

Transfer the mince mixture to a 30 cm × 23 cm roasting tin and pour over 875 ml (3½ cups) of the boiling water. Scatter over the parsley, then transfer to the oven and cook for 30 minutes.

Remove the tin from the oven and stir and fluff the rice with a fork. If the rice appears dry, add the remaining boiling water. Return to the oven and cook for a further 15 minutes, until the rice is tender.

Zoe Konikkos,
Victoria

Makaronia tou fournou

Cypriot-style pastitsio

Growing up, I spent the majority of my time at Yiayia and Bapou's house. My love for cooking and fresh produce stems from spending much of my life watching or cooking with Yiayia, under the watchful eye of Bapou. Yiayia taught me everything I know about food.

As a child, there was nothing better than getting home from school and walking into Yiayia's house. You just knew you were going to get something special. For me, that special something was her makaronia tou fournou – a Cypriot baked pasta dish, filled with spiced mince and topped with a halloumi bechamel. I knew before I'd even opened the front door what she was going to cook for dinner that night. I'd smell the spices wafting outside as I walked up the porch steps and I'd start telling myself, 'No after-school snacks – save some space for the good stuff!' Yiayia would make the biggest pot of bechamel (my favourite part!) and I remember sitting on the kitchen floor between her feet licking the pot clean.

Among the countless dishes she has taught me, which I've eaten with her or that she has cooked for me, this is truly the one that feels like home. It's the one that always takes me back to her kitchen floor and the dish that I will continue to cook for my children and grandchildren for years to come. Even though I've added a few personal touches, it's my way of having her with me always.

SERVES 8–10

3–4 tablespoons extra-virgin
   olive oil
1 onion, diced
300 g beef mince
300 g pork mince
1 teaspoon ground cinnamon
⅛ teaspoon ground cloves
⅛ teaspoon ground nutmeg
185 g (¾ cup) passata
salt and black pepper, to taste
500 g dried penne

Continued overleaf →

Preheat the oven to 180°C (160°C fan-forced) and grease a large baking dish with oil.

Heat the olive oil in a large heavy-based saucepan over medium–high heat. Add the onion and cook for about 5 minutes, until translucent. Add the minces and cook, breaking up any lumps with the back of a wooden spoon, for 8–10 minutes, until browned. Add the cinnamon, clove and nutmeg and stir until well combined, then add the passata and 3 tablespoons of water. Reduce the heat to a simmer and cook for 10–15 minutes, until slightly thickened. Season to taste with salt and pepper.

Meanwhile, bring a large saucepan of salted water to the boil over medium–high heat and add the penne. Cook for 7–8 minutes until almost al dente, then drain and transfer to the baking dish. Pour the meat sauce over the penne and stir to combine.

Halloumi bechamel

150 g salted butter
150 g (1 cup) plain flour
1 litre full-cream milk
110 g (¾ cup) grated halloumi,
    plus extra for sprinkling
60 g (½ cup) grated cheddar
25 g (¼ cup) grated parmesan
⅛ teaspoon ground nutmeg
salt and black pepper

To make the halloumi bechamel, melt the butter in a saucepan over medium heat. Add the flour and whisk for 3–4 minutes, until the mixture thickens and resembles wet sand. Gradually add the milk, 500 ml (2 cups) at a time, whisking constantly to stop lumps forming, until thickened. Bring to a gentle boil, then remove from the heat and whisk in all the cheese, the nutmeg and salt and pepper to taste.

Spread the bechamel over the pasta and meat sauce in a thick layer, then transfer to the oven and cook for 40 minutes or until bubbling and golden.

Mum's cannelloni

This dish is very close to Yiayia's heart, as it was taught to her by our mum, Teresa. Like Yiayia, Mum had a fondness for cooking and, more importantly, for making sure we were always well fed and cared for. One of the many things we miss about our mum is her cooking. We are very fortunate that she passed this recipe on to Yiayia, so we can still enjoy it to this day and help fill the void in our hearts.

SERVES 4

500 g fresh ricotta,
  plus extra to serve
3 eggs, beaten
1 small bunch of flat-leaf
  parsley, roughly chopped
  (Yiayia always uses scissors),
  plus extra to serve
1 garlic clove, finely chopped
½ teaspoon salt
250 g dried cannelloni
700 g jar passata
150 g shredded mozzarella

Preheat the oven to 190°C (170°C fan-forced).

Place the ricotta in a large bowl and use a fork to break it up. Add the egg, parsley, garlic and salt and gently mix with a spoon until well combined.

Using a small teaspoon, fill the cannelloni with the ricotta mixture, then place the filled cannelloni in a 30 cm × 20 cm baking dish in a single layer. Evenly pour the passata over the top, then sprinkle over the mozzarella, transfer to the oven and bake for 55 minutes or until the cannelloni are cooked through and the sauce is bubbling.

Serve with extra ricotta and parsley scattered over the top.

Nonna Rosa loves our mum's cannelloni, see page 97

Thalassina & Kreatika

Seafood & Meat

Mary Kalifatidis,
Victoria

Psari kleftiko

Baked fish parcels

When I was growing up, my mum would often cook a whole fish in the oven with some veggies. I distinctly remember my three younger sisters and I constantly complaining about eating fish with bones. Having previously swallowed a few fishbones here and there, the fear was real. It would often take us a good hour to slowly and carefully swallow each bite, by which time our dinners would be cold. We'd chew the fish from side to side until it was dry and tasteless, but eventually you'd find the bones. If we did accidentally swallow one my mother would simply tell us to eat the ends of crusty bread to push the bone down.

Certain foods and meals trigger emotions and feelings, and the taste, smell and texture of that fish is so vivid and clear in my memory that I found myself needing to recreate it, but with more flavour and definitely no bones. Simple changes, such as caramelising the onions, peppers and garlic, added sweetness to the dish, while spices and herbs added more depth and flavour to the fish. In today's world there are so many ingredients available that allow the home cook to become a master chef, and inspire the next generation to cook and eat and bring people together.

I like to serve this fish with a simple salad of shredded red cabbage, chopped kale and roasted sunflower seeds. Toss through with your favourite dressing.

SERVES 6

1 tablespoon olive oil
20 g butter
3 large onions, roughly chopped
2 red bullhorn peppers (or capsicums), roughly chopped
2 garlic cloves, crushed
1 bunch of flat-leaf parsley, chopped
salt and black pepper
6 x 250 g firm white fish fillets, such as cod, rockling or John Dory
1 teaspoon smoked paprika, for sprinkling
1 teaspoon dried oregano, for sprinkling
balsamic glaze, for drizzling
pinch of chilli flakes (optional)

Preheat the oven to 180°C (160°C fan-forced).

Heat the olive oil and butter in a large frying pan over medium heat. Add the onion and cook for about 5 minutes, until soft and translucent, then add the pepper and cook for 5–8 minutes, until starting to caramelise. Add the garlic and cook for 1–2 minutes, until fragrant, then add the parsley and cook, stirring, for 2 minutes. Season with salt and pepper, then remove from the heat and set aside.

Sprinkle both sides of the fish fillets with paprika, oregano, salt and pepper to taste.

Tear off six squares of baking paper large enough to wrap each fish fillet individually. Place a fish fillet in the centre of each square of baking paper, then evenly spoon the cooked onion and pepper mixture over the fish. Drizzle a little balsamic glaze over the top and finish with a few chilli flakes (if desired). Fold over the top and sides of each baking paper square to form a well-sealed pouch, then transfer to a large baking tray. Bake for 15–20 minutes (the cooking time will depend on the thickness of the fish), until the fish is opaque and just cooked through. Divide the fish parcels among plates and serve with your choice of sides.

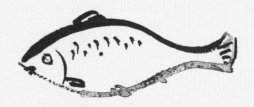

Psari plaki me kremmidi & patates

Baked fish with onion & potato

One day, Yiayia was inspired to cook a healthier alternative to fried fish. She created this recipe, baking salmon with onion and potato in the same dish. Pappou says it is very tasty and recommends that you try it. He also likes that there is only one dish to wash up.

SERVES 4

3 tablespoons canola or olive oil
4 large onions, finely sliced
2 large potatoes, peeled and finely sliced
2 teaspoons ground paprika
1 teaspoon salt
4 x 150 g salmon or blue grenadier fillets, skin on
crusty bread or salad, to serve

Preheat the oven to 180°C (160°C fan-forced).

Heat the oil in a flameproof casserole dish over low heat. Add the onion and gently cook for 3 minutes. Add the potato, paprika, salt and 375 ml (1½ cups) of water and bring to the boil, stirring occasionally. Cover the dish with a lid, transfer to the oven and bake for 30 minutes, removing the lid halfway through.

Add the fish, skin-side down, to the dish, then return to the oven and bake for 15–20 minutes or until the fish is just cooked through.

Divide the fish and potato among plates and serve with your choice of crusty bread or salad.

Philip Vakos,
Victoria

Kotopoulo fricassee me agginares

Chicken & artichoke fricassee

This fricassee has a special place in my heart. It is the pinnacle of what I consider to be comfort food. I remember getting home from school and my yiayia telling me to go to the 'kipo' (garden) and collect some produce for dinner. She would either make this chicken and artichoke fricassee, or a pork and celery version. As we had an abundance of chickens running around (as you do!) and heaps of artichokes growing, it became a standard dish that we enjoyed a few times a week. Cleaning the artichokes was easy; cleaning the chicken on the other hand ... well you can use your imagination. The end result was always magic, and now it's a dish I bring out every winter at my restaurant. A comforting, creamy, zesty chicken stew with chunky artichokes ... I mean, what's not to love about it?!

SERVES 4–6

50 ml olive oil
2 large onions, finely chopped
1 fennel bulb, diced
2 kg chicken marylands
1 cup (loosely packed) dill
 fronds, finely chopped,
 plus extra to serve
2 tablespoons sea salt flakes
1 litre chicken stock or water,
 plus extra if needed
freshly ground black pepper
2 lemons, halved
6 globe artichokes, stalks
 trimmed to 5 cm
2 eggs
25 g cornflour
crusty bread, to serve

Heat the oil in a large flameproof casserole dish over medium–high heat. Add the onion and fennel and cook for 4–5 minutes, until soft and translucent. Add the chicken and sear for 3–4 minutes, until browned all over, then add the dill, salt and chicken stock or water. You want to just cover the chicken, so add a little extra stock or water if necessary. Season to taste with pepper, then bring to the boil, reduce the heat to low and simmer for 10–15 minutes, until the chicken is just tender.

Meanwhile, fill a large bowl with cold water. Squeeze in the juice from two of the lemon halves, adding the spent lemon halves as well. Working with one artichoke at a time, remove the tough outer leaves, then trim the top and peel the stalk. Halve lengthways, then use a teaspoon to scrape out the fibrous heart and discard. Rub the cut sides with one of the remaining lemon halves, then place the artichoke in the acidulated water. Repeat with the remaining artichokes.

When the chicken is just tender, increase the heat to medium. Drain the artichokes, add to the dish and cook for 4–5 minutes, until tender.

Meanwhile, whisk the eggs, the juice from the remaining lemon halves and the cornflour in a bowl. Whisk in 500 ml (2 cups) of the chicken stock, ladle by ladle, then pour the mixture into the dish and stir to combine. Gently bring to the boil, then immediately remove from the heat. Season generously to taste, then transfer the fricassee to a serving dish.

Serve in shallow bowls, with crusty bread to mop up the lemony juices.

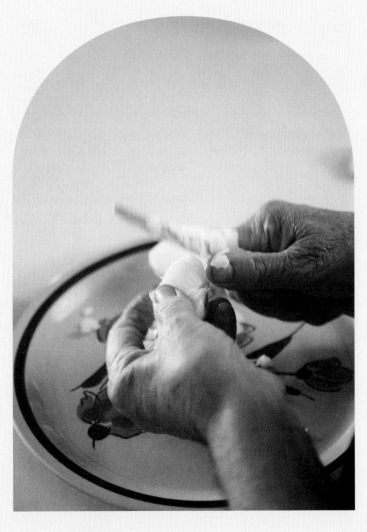

Kotopoulo me rizi

Chicken & rice

This was the first dish Yiayia passed over the fence! Truly the start of something special.

It's clear from our Instagram feed that this is everyone's favourite dish from Yiayia (and ours too). Typically on a plate wrapped in foil, it's the equivalent of unwrapping a present early on Christmas morning. Like all transactions over the fence, Yiayia calls our mobile and we ecstatically answer her request to 'come outside Daniel and Lucas'.

SERVES 3–4

6 chicken drumsticks
200 g (1 cup) medium-grain rice
1 onion, finely chopped
2 tablespoons olive oil
pinch of salt and black pepper

Preheat the oven to 180°C (160°C fan-forced).

Wash and pat dry the chicken drumsticks, then transfer to a large saucepan and cover with plenty of water. Bring to the boil over high heat, then immediately reduce the heat to a very low simmer, cover and cook for 20 minutes, occasionally skimming off any foam that rises to the surface.

Remove the chicken drumsticks from the pan and strain the stock into a bowl, reserving 500 ml (2 cups). Pour the stock into a 25 cm × 20 cm baking dish, then add the rice, onion, oil and salt and pepper to taste. Transfer to the oven and cook for 30 minutes.

Place the poached drumsticks on top of the rice, then return to the oven and cook for a further 15 minutes, until the chicken is lightly golden and cooked through and the rice is tender.

Divide among plates and serve.

Kotopoulo me rizi (chicken & rice), see page 108

Moshari me fasolakia

Beef, bean & potato stew

When Yiayia was a young girl, her parents and siblings worked at the local farm. One day Yiayia came home from school and decided to surprise her family with a cooked meal. She made this dish using generous amounts of olive oil. Her father loved it and complimented Yiayia's cooking, but her mother questioned the amount of oil she had used. Yiayia was scolded for using a few days' supply of oil for one dish.

Serves 4

80 ml (⅓ cup) canola oil
1 large onion, diced
4 red peppers (or capsicums), diced
440 g fillet beef topside, cut into 10 pieces
2 teaspoons salt
1 tablespoon ground paprika
1.5 litres boiling water
600 g green beans, topped and tailed
5 large desiree potatoes, peeled and cut into bite-sized pieces
crusty bread, to serve

Heat the oil in a large saucepan over medium–high heat. Add the onion and pepper and cook for 3–4 minutes or until soft. Add the beef and brown on all sides for about 5 minutes. Add the salt and paprika, stir to coat, then pour in the boiling water. Add the beans and potato and bring to the boil, then cover and cook over medium heat for 30 minutes.

Serve the stew with crusty bread to mop up all the delicious juices.

Sikotakia kotopoulo

Chicken livers

'Be careful!' warns Pappou. Yiayia has burned herself many times cooking livers, as they sizzle and splatter like crazy when frying. A simple dish from a simpler time, Yiayia likes to serve this with rice and a fresh grilled pepper salad (see page 142).

SERVES 2

20 chicken livers, cleaned and trimmed
salt
2 tablespoons canola oil

Half-fill a saucepan with water and bring to the boil over high heat. Add the livers and boil for 15 minutes or until light brown and soft, then drain and season well with salt.

Heat the oil in a frying pan with a lid over medium heat. Gently lay the chicken livers in the pan and cover, leaving the lid slightly ajar. Cook for 2 minutes, then turn the livers over (Yiayia uses the lid as a shield when doing this as the livers pop like popcorn). Continue to cook the livers, partially covered, for 4–5 minutes, until golden brown. Transfer to a plate lined with paper towel to drain.

Serve with your choice of sides or salad.

Lahanohirino stifado

Cabbage & pork stew

Yiayia's parents grew cabbages in Florina, the village where she grew up. They were harvested in summer and stored in a cool place to eat over the following months. This stew brings back happy memories for her.

SERVES 4

3 pork loin chops
3 tablespoons extra-virgin olive oil
3 small onions, cut into large chunks
1½ teaspoons ground paprika
1 teaspoon salt
1.25 litres boiling water
2 dried red chillies
½ green cabbage, cut into 3 cm chunks

Begin by cutting each pork chop into three even pieces.

Heat the oil in a large saucepan over high heat, add the onion and cook for about 2 minutes, until just starting to brown. Reduce the heat to medium, add the pork and cook, stirring occasionally, for 2 minutes. Add the paprika and salt and stir until fragrant, then add the boiling water and gently stir. Increase the heat to high and add the dried chillies, then cover and allow to boil for 9 minutes. Reduce the heat to medium, leave the lid slightly ajar and continue to cook for a further 35 minutes or until the pork is cooked through.

Remove the pork from the pan and set aside to rest, covered with foil. Increase the heat to high, add three handfuls of cabbage and cook, pressing down, until starting to collapse. Continue to add the cabbage, pressing down after each addition, until it's all added. Reduce the heat to medium, then cover and cook, pressing down every 5 minutes, for 10 minutes, until the cabbage is completely collapsed and tender. Return the pork to the pan for the final 2 minutes of cooking to heat through.

Divide the pork and cabbage among plates and serve.

Keftedes

Meatballs

Yiayia receives many requests from her children and their friends for her famous meatballs. They are loved and devoured by everyone and it's almost impossible to stop at just one or two.

SERVES 4–6

250 g pork mince
250 g beef mince
1 egg
1 teaspoon salt
1 tablespoon dried oregano
50 g (½ cup) dried breadcrumbs
1 tablespoon olive oil
handful of chopped flat-leaf
    parsley
canola oil, for shallow-frying

Place all the ingredients except the canola oil in a large bowl. Using clean hands, massage and squeeze the ingredients for 5–10 minutes, until completely combined and homogenous. Cover and refrigerate for 30 minutes or up to 1 hour if you have time.

Divide the mixture into even portions and roll into walnut-sized balls, then slightly flatten. You should get about 18 balls.

Heat enough canola oil for shallow-frying in a large frying pan over medium–high heat. Working in batches, cook the meatballs for 2–3 minutes on all sides, until cooked through and golden brown. Enjoy!

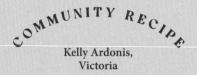
Kelly Ardonis,
Victoria

Katina's moussaka

My dear mother, Katina, who is a grandmother to two grandchildren, two fur children and a mother of three proud kids, used to cook such amazing, inviting dishes that brought an abundance of happy times to our family, friends and neighbourhood.

I have fond memories of baking and cooking with my niece, sister and mum in our family home. We prepared Greek dishes, such as spanakopita, tiropita, fasolakia, keftedes, yemista, pastitsio, xorta, moussaka, koulourakia, melomakarona, kourabiethes, to name a few. Koulourakia was always a special recipe – Mum would encourage us to 'make extra' so we could share some with our neighbours. She taught me to respect the elderly and people living alone around us. Avgolemono soup is a dish Mum also prepared when anyone was unwell or needed something comforting and warming to eat.

When I was younger, my mum, dad and I used to go foraging around Melbourne for wild mushrooms and earthy greens to cook and bake with – something that used to embarrass me. I also remember my primary-school years, when Mum used to make morning, lunch and, sometimes, afternoon meals for me and walk them down to the school to share with the other kids and teachers. Again, embarrassing at the time, but so very special to think back on those memories now.

My mum was diagnosed with early onset vascular dementia 18 months ago, and she is now in the wonderful care of a Greek nursing home. She still gets around to cooking with support, and helps staff and volunteers around her, including making koulourakia for the homeless. She is and forever will be my biggest inspiration and drive in life; she has opened her heart to so many, and brings so much joy to all who meet her.

Every time I cook, I think of her. Every time I help someone in my day, I think of her. Seeing the Yiayia Next Door Instagram posts and community spirit, I also think of her. I have shown her some of these posts and she says, 'what a great Yiayia to look after the boys'.

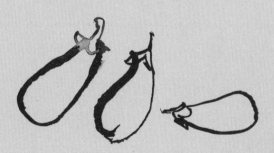

3 eggplants, cut lengthways
  into 5 mm thick slices
4 zucchini, cut lengthways
  into 5 mm thick slices
4 potatoes, peeled and cut
  into 5 mm thick slices
2 tablespoons olive oil,
  plus extra for brushing
salt and black pepper
1 onion, finely chopped
1 carrot, finely chopped
1 celery stalk, finely chopped
2 garlic cloves, finely chopped
1 kg beef mince
400 g can crushed tomatoes
1 tablespoon tomato paste
1 tablespoon sugar
4 dried bay leaves
2 teaspoons ground cinnamon,
  plus extra for sprinkling
1 tablespoon vegetable
  stock powder
120 g (1 cup) grated
  kefalograviera cheese,
  plus extra for sprinkling
salad, to serve

Traditional bechamel

500 ml (2 cups) full-cream milk
60 g unsalted butter
55 g (⅓ cup) fine semolina
120 g (1 cup) grated
  kefalograviera cheese
salt and black pepper

Preheat the oven to 180°C (160°C fan-forced).

Place the eggplant, zucchini and potato slices on separate large baking trays in single layers. Brush both sides of the vegetable slices with olive oil and season with salt and pepper to taste. Transfer to the oven and cook, turning the vegetables over halfway through the cooking time, for 20–25 minutes, until tender.

Meanwhile, heat the olive oil in a large saucepan over medium heat. Add the onion, carrot, celery and garlic and cook for about 10 minutes, until soft and lightly golden. Increase the heat to medium–high, add the mince and cook, breaking up any lumps with the back of a wooden spoon, for 7–8 minutes, until browned. Add the tomatoes, then half-fill the can with water, give it a swirl and add the liquid to the pan. Stir through the tomato paste, sugar, bay leaves, cinnamon and stock powder and season with salt and pepper to taste. Reduce the heat to low and cook for about 30 minutes, until reduced and thick. Remove and discard the bay leaves.

To make the bechamel, heat the milk and butter in a saucepan over medium–low heat. Once the butter has melted, slowly add the semolina in a steady stream, whisking constantly, for 2–3 minutes, until the mixture boils and thickens. Remove from the heat and stir through the kefalograviera cheese until melted and the bechamel is thick. Season to taste with salt and pepper.

To assemble the moussaka, spoon a thin layer of bechamel into the base of a 33 cm × 26 cm baking dish. Add the baked eggplant slices followed by the baked potato slices, then sprinkle over half the kefalograviera cheese. Add all the mince mixture, followed by the remaining kefalograviera cheese, then top with the baked zucchini slices. Finish with the remaining bechamel, spreading it out in an even layer. Sprinkle with extra kefalograviera cheese and a little ground cinnamon, then transfer to the oven and cook for 25–30 minutes, until bubbling and the top is golden brown. If you would like to brown the bechamel even more, flash it under a hot grill for about 8 minutes.

Set aside to rest for 40 minutes before slicing and serving with your choice of salad. See overleaf for the finished dish.

Note

Mum always saved the bechamel pan and spoon for those who helped her prepare. Scraping the leftover sauce was the best part.

Katina's moussaka, see page 118

Paidakia tis skaras

Marinated lamb cutlets

This was one of the first dishes Yiayia learned from her mum and yiayia in Meliti, Greece. The dish means a lot to Yiayia's family because they always cooked it together at celebrations, and it has been passed down through the generations. Yiayia loves to share this dish with others as she gets a kick out of seeing people's reactions when they eat her family's famous lamb cutlets. It reminds her of all the great memories they shared growing up.

As Yiayia always says when passing a plate wrapped in foil over the fence: 'I hope you like it!' And we guarantee you will.

SERVES 4

3–4 tablespoons extra-virgin olive oil
6 garlic cloves, left whole or roughly chopped
3 tablespoons chopped oregano leaves (or 2 tablespoons dried oregano)
½ bunch of thyme, leaves picked
juice of 2 lemons
1–2 teaspoons salt
1–2 teaspoons black pepper
pinch of ground paprika
1 tablespoon rosemary leaves
8 lamb cutlets, trimmed

Combine all the ingredients except the lamb cutlets in a large shallow baking dish. Add the lamb cutlets and turn to coat in the marinade. Cover and set aside in the fridge for 2–3 hours, but ideally overnight.

Remove the lamb cutlets from the fridge and bring to room temperature for 1 hour before cooking.

Heat a large frying pan over medium–high heat. Working in batches, add the lamb cutlets and cook for 2–3 minutes each side (depending on their thickness), until just cooked through. Allow to rest for a few minutes before serving with your choice of sides.

Lahano dolmades

Cabbage rolls

Yiayia had her own recipe for cabbage rolls, but when her late sister, Menka, came to visit from Belgium she taught Yiayia this version. Yiayia says her sister's recipe was better than her own, so now she makes this one instead. It holds a special place in Yiayia's heart.

SERVES 4–6

1 large green cabbage, leaves separated
boiling water
80 ml (⅓ cup) olive oil
1 onion, finely chopped
500 g mince (half beef topside, half pork fillet, minced twice; ask your butcher to do this for you)
250 g (1¼ cups) medium-grain rice, rinsed
1 teaspoon ground paprika
1 teaspoon dried oregano
1½ teaspoons salt
lemon wedges, to serve

Cut the hard core out of the bottom of each cabbage leaf. Place the cabbage leaves in a large saucepan and pour over enough boiling water to completely cover them. Set aside.

Heat the oil in a large frying pan over medium heat. Add the onion and cook for about 5 minutes, until soft and translucent. Increase the heat to medium–high, add the mince and cook, breaking up any lumps with the back of a wooden spoon, for about 7 minutes, until well browned. Remove the pan from the heat and stir through the rice.

Return the pan to medium heat and stir through the paprika, oregano and salt. Cook for 2 minutes or until fragrant, then remove from the heat again.

Drain the cabbage. Place a handful of the mince mixture and a few loose cabbage leaves in the base of the now-empty saucepan. Place one of the remaining cabbage leaves, vein-side down (it should be about the size of your hand), on a clean work surface and top with 1 heaped tablespoon of the remaining mince mixture. Fold in the sides of the cabbage leaf, then tightly roll up into a parcel, squeezing out any liquid. Transfer to the base of the saucepan, on top of the loose cabbage leaves. Repeat with the remaining cabbage leaves and mince mixture to make about 20 cabbage rolls, fitting them snugly in the saucepan as you go (you'll end up with at least two layers of cabbage rolls). Pour enough boiling water into the pan to just cover the cabbage rolls, then cover with a lid, place over medium heat and cook for 30 minutes, until the rice is tender.

Remove the pan from the heat and allow to cool slightly. Transfer the cabbage rolls to a serving plate and serve with lemon wedges for squeezing over.

Mum's rack of lamb with jam

This was one of the first dishes we all learned to cook – and perfect – with Mum, so it means a lot to us. Whenever Mum asked us what we wanted her to make for a special occasion the answer was always the same. It is one of the last meals she cooked for us, requested by Daniel for his twenty-third birthday. We will always remember it, as her legacy lives on through us and in our hearts forever. Mum would be so proud to share this with you all – we hope you enjoy it as much as we do!

SERVES 4–6

2 Frenched lamb racks
2 teaspoons extra-virgin olive oil
6 garlic cloves, left whole or chopped
½ bunch of rosemary, leaves picked
160 g (½ cup) strawberry jam
juice of 1 lemon
250 ml (1 cup) red wine (preferably cabernet sauvignon or shiraz)
1–2 tablespoons salt
1 tablespoon black pepper
1 teaspoon stock powder (any kind)
your choice of salad or vegetables, to serve

Allow the lamb to come to room temperature for 1 hour before cooking.

Preheat the oven to 180°C (160°C fan-forced).

Heat the oil in a large frying pan over medium–high heat. Working with one rack at a time, sear the racks for 2 minutes each side or until browned.

Meanwhile, combine the remaining ingredients, except the stock powder, in a large baking dish. Transfer the seared lamb to the dish, turning to coat the lamb in the sauce. Carefully wrap each section of bone in foil to avoid burning, then transfer to the oven and cook for 20 minutes.

Turn the lamb racks over and add 250 ml (1 cup) of water and the stock powder to the jam sauce (this prevents the sauce from drying out). Return to the oven and cook for a further 20 minutes.

Allow the lamb racks to rest, covered, for 10 minutes, then transfer to a serving dish and serve with your choice of salad or vegetables.

Enjoying mum's rack of lamb with jam (see page 126) with Nonna Rosa

Katherine Nikolakoudis,
Victoria

Kokkinisto

Greek-style ragu

This is a simple pasta sauce that we used to request whenever we visited my yiayia and pappou. Yiayia loved cooking for the family, and over the years her daughters (my aunties) have tried to replicate this dish. There must have been something special about Yiayia's pots, her magic touch and the love she put into every meal because no one has ever quite nailed it.

Yiayia would cook pasta to serve with this sauce, and her secret to making it even tastier was to sprinkle some mizithra cheese on the bottom of each plate, then top with the pasta and sauce and then sprinkle more cheese on top. Fresh bread was always on the table to dip into the sauce, too.

SERVES 4–6

1–2 tablespoons olive oil
1–2 large onions, diced
1 kg meat of your choice, such as chuck steak or boneless lamb, cut into chunks, or cutlets on the bone (skin off)
1 teaspoon ground cloves
1 teaspoon ground cinnamon
pinch of freshly grated nutmeg
1 tablespoon tomato paste
350 g passata
salt and black pepper
boiling water
cooked rigatoni or spiral pasta, steamed rice or homemade thick chips, to serve

Heat the oil in a large saucepan over medium heat, add the onion and cook for about 5 minutes, until soft and translucent. Add the meat and cook for 10 minutes or until seared on all sides. Add the clove, cinnamon and nutmeg and cook, stirring, for 1–2 minutes, until fragrant, then stir through the tomato paste and passata. Season with salt and pepper to taste and add enough boiling water to just cover the meat. Bring the mixture to the boil, then reduce the heat to low and cook for about 2½ hours (or 15–20 minutes if using chicken), until the meat is tender and the sauce has thickened.

Serve with cooked pasta, steamed rice or homemade thick chips.

Salates & Lahanika

Salads & Vegetables

Piperies tis skaras

Grilled peppers

Paying homage to the way she was raised, to live off the land, Yiayia uses home-grown peppers from her garden to make this dish. She says they have a different taste to the peppers you buy in the supermarket. Yiayia encourages everyone to grow their own produce.

SERVES 2–3

13 mixed red and green bullhorn
  peppers (or capsicums)
olive oil, for drizzling
salt

Preheat the grill to high.

Place the peppers under the grill and cook, turning frequently, for 15–20 minutes, until soft and semi-charred on all sides. Transfer the peppers to a large zip-lock bag as they finish cooking, then seal the bag and set aside for the peppers to steam and cool.

The process of peeling the peppers is most important. Starting at the stem of each pepper, begin peeling the skin by first tearing it horizontally and then peeling vertically. To open up the peppers, gently insert your thumb and run it down the inside to remove the seeds and membrane. Discard the seeds and membranes, remove the stems, then transfer the peppers to a serving plate.

Drizzle a good amount of olive oil over the peppers, season with salt to taste and serve.

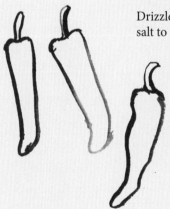

Piperies tis skaras (grilled peppers), see page 138

Garden salad, Yiayia style

Using scissors, cut six grilled peppers (see page 138) into bite-sized pieces, then transfer to a salad bowl. Add two diced tomatoes, one sliced Lebanese cucumber and one finely chopped garlic clove and mix well to combine. Drizzle with good-quality Greek olive oil, season to taste with salt and serve.

Crystal Marie Vicario,
Victoria

Patates lemonates

Lemon potatoes

This recipe is one I hold very close to my heart. Patates lemonates is a comforting dish that I grew up with and makes me feel all warm and fuzzy. When I think of childhood memories, I always think back to Sundays and how they were the most significant day of the week for me. Sunday, the day of rest. Coming from a single-parent family, Mum had to work a lot. To me, Sundays meant that she'd be home, and it was our day to feast together as a family.

Mum would get up in the early hours of the morning to start making the Sunday roast, along with everyone's favourite: patates lemonates. The aromas of lemon, garlic and cinnamon would waft through the house (and neighbourhood!) as my older siblings and I would begin to wake up. It was heaven! We would always demolish the zesty tray of lemon potatoes first. The best part was dunking pieces of fresh bread into all the crispy juices left in the tray ... Delicious!

This recipe was passed down from my yiayia, who was from the Greek island of Léros. Now that I'm a mother, I'm so grateful and blessed that I get to continue the tradition with my children, Elijah and Ruby, creating new memories and bringing them the same joy that this dish brought me. Best of all, it contains no gluten or dairy and is 100 per cent vegan so absolutely anyone can gather round to enjoy it!

SERVES 3–4

6 roasting potatoes (I use red royale), peeled and quartered lengthways
4 garlic cloves, roughly chopped
½ teaspoon dried Greek mountain oregano
¼ teaspoon ground cinnamon
½ teaspoon sweet paprika
1 teaspoon vegan chicken-style stock powder
juice of 2 lemons
125 ml (½ cup) extra-virgin olive oil

Preheat the oven to 200°C (180°C fan-forced).

Place the potato in a large bowl and add the garlic, oregano, cinnamon, paprika and stock powder. Toss to combine, then pour in the lemon juice, olive oil and 500 ml (2 cups) of water and mix well.

Using a slotted spoon, transfer the potato to a non-stick roasting tin and pour the lemony liquid over the top. Cover with foil and bake for 40 minutes.

Remove the foil, add another 250 ml (1 cup) of water if the tray is nearly dry and carefully tilt the tray from side to side so the liquid is evenly distributed. Bake for a further 30 minutes or until the potato is tender and golden.

Lahanika toursi

Pickled vegetables

Yiayia always keeps a jar of pickled vegetables in her fridge as, apart from being delicious, she thinks they're the best cure for car sickness. Yiayia picks vegetables from her garden when they are ripe and pickles them for her and Pappou to enjoy later in the year.

MAKES 2 KG

750 g green cabbage, torn into 3 cm pieces
750 g green bullhorn peppers (or capsicums), roughly chopped
500 g green tomatoes, quartered

Pickling brine

250 ml (1 cup) white vinegar
2 tablespoons salt
1 tablespoon sugar

To make the pickling brine, combine the ingredients and 750 ml (3 cups) of water in a non-reactive bowl and stir until the salt and sugar are dissolved.

Stuff two large or four smaller sterilised jars (see Note) tightly with the vegetables, then pour the brine over the vegetables, ensuring they are completely submerged. Screw the lids on tightly, then set aside in a cool, dark place for 10 days before serving. The vegetables should be soft and lightly pickled.

Once open, transfer the jar to the fridge, where the pickled veg will keep for up to 6 months.

Note

To sterilise jars, wash the jars and lids in hot, soapy water and rinse well, or run them through a hot cycle in the dishwasher. Leave to air-dry on a clean tea towel.

Poure me kokkines piperies

Dried red pepper mash

At the end of summer, Yiayia harvests the remaining peppers in her garden, threads them together with cotton and hangs them up to dry to use throughout the rest of the year. This dish is one of Yiayia's winter favourites. Served with crusty bread, Yiayia says red pepper mash is 'finger lickin' Yiayia good'.

SERVES 6

7 small-to-medium desiree potatoes, peeled and sliced 1 cm thick
100 g dried red bullhorn peppers (or capsicums; see Note), washed and drained
1 dried red chilli (if you can handle the heat!)
1 tablespoon olive oil
¼ teaspoon chilli flakes
1½ teaspoons salt
½ garlic clove, finely chopped (optional)
crusty bread, to serve

Layer the potato evenly in the base of a large saucepan and place the peppers and chilli (if using) on top. Position a saucer over the peppers, then pour in 1.5 litres of cold water (the saucer will stop the peppers and chilli floating to the top). Bring to the boil over high heat, then reduce the heat to medium and cook, covered but with the lid slightly ajar, for 35 minutes or until the potato and peppers are very soft and cooked through. Drain, then carefully pull the cores from the peppers and chilli and discard.

Transfer the potato and peppers to a clean saucepan and, using a wooden spoon, mash the ingredients together, using the back of the spoon to tear the peppers and chilli into small pieces. Add the oil, chilli flakes, salt and garlic (if desired) and continue to mash until smooth and well combined.

Transfer to a bowl and serve with crusty bread.

Note

To dry bullhorn peppers or capsicums, use a thick needle and a long piece of thread to tie the peppers together in a long line. Hang the peppers in a cool, dry spot indoors for about 1 week, until completely dry. Alternatively, if you have a dehydrator, follow the manufacturer's instructions to dehydrate the peppers. Store in an airtight container in the pantry for up to 3 months.

Pappou's Garden Tips

Pappou takes great pride in his garden, so protecting it from predators is a top priority. You'll also find many common household items enjoying a second life outside. Here are Pappou's top tips.

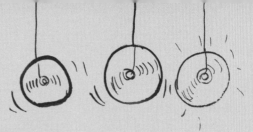

1 Pappou uses old shoelaces to help support baby plants by gently tying them to wooden stakes.

2 Pappou hangs old milk containers or crates over newly planted cucumbers to protect them from direct sunlight. Once the plants are too big to cover, replace the containers or crates with mesh or anything else that can provide a bit of shade.

3 Did you know cucumbers are a vine? This is why they want to grab onto things as they grow, so it's a great idea to plant them up against a piece of metal mesh to give them plenty of room to spread and hang.

4 To keep cats and possums at bay, Pappou places water-filled glass bottles, jars or even plastic bottles (as long as they're clear) around the garden. When cats or possums walk past, they are scared away by their own reflection.

5 To scare off hungry birds and bats, hang old CDs or children's toys in your fruit trees. Pappou likes to put nets around his fruit trees, too.

6 When growing tomatoes, let your plants develop strong main branches, then trim off any smaller branches that sprout from them. Keep doing this as your tomatoes grow – this lets the plants focus their energy on the large branches and produce more fruit for you. Oh, and Pappou recommends watering your tomatoes early in the morning and then again at night in summer.

7 Pappou fully supports the myth that peeing on citrus trees while they're growing is good for them, so go ahead, boys. Putting rusty nails at the base of a citrus tree also works.

8 If a particular fruit or vegetable is growing well in your veggie patch, make sure to save some of its seeds for replanting. Dry out the seeds and label them for the next planting season.

9 Reuse old jars to grow seeds and seedlings inside before transplanting them in the garden.

Potato wedges, Yiayia style

Preheat the oven to 200°C (180°C fan-forced). Peel five large desiree potatoes and slice them into 1 cm thick wedges. Scatter into a large roasting tin in a single layer, then sprinkle with salt and drizzle over some olive oil. Transfer to the oven and cook for 30 minutes. Turn the wedges over, drizzle with a little more oil and continue to cook for 15–20 minutes or until the wedges are cooked through and golden.

Bamies

Okra, tomato & potato casserole

My Aunty Pam lived next door to us throughout my childhood. She was older than my mother and was like my yiayia. I would go next door every morning before school and eat breakfast, and every afternoon for cake and milk or whatever was cooking. Those years were the best times of my life, knowing that my neighbour/aunty/yiayia was always there and loved me so much. Through her I learned how to cook Greek food, and now I love feeding anyone who visits. My favourite dish of hers was bamies (okra). I loved this slimy vegetable and I would wipe the bowl clean with crusty bread.

My aunty now has severe dementia and she lives in a nursing home along with her husband, Jim (my uncle). When the dementia started she cried knowing that she would forget her recipes and wouldn't be able to cook anymore. Food was her way of showing love. I am so grateful for growing up next door to Pam and Jim, and I will never forget the love I felt. They would always walk me to the front gate to say goodbye and watch me walk home next door. They are the most loving souls. They give love through food and I wish I could have just one more visit next door.

SERVES 4–6

500 g fresh or frozen and thawed okra, stalks removed
125 ml (½ cup) white wine vinegar
125 ml (½ cup) olive oil
4–5 all-purpose potatoes, peeled and cut into bite-sized wedges
2 onions, chopped
2 garlic cloves, chopped
1–2 tablespoons tomato paste
2 x 400 g cans chopped tomatoes
½ teaspoon sugar
1 tablespoon dried oregano
1 bay leaf
salt and black pepper
½ bunch of dill or flat-leaf parsley, chopped
crumbled feta, to serve (optional)
crusty bread, to serve

Place the okra in a large non-reactive bowl, pour over the vinegar and add enough water to just cover the okra. Set aside for 30 minutes, then drain and pat dry with paper towel.

Heat the olive oil in a flameproof casserole dish over medium heat, add the potato and cook for 5 minutes. Add the onion and garlic and fry for 2 minutes until fragrant, then add the tomato paste, tomatoes, sugar, oregano, bay leaf and 250 ml (1 cup) of water. Season with salt and pepper to taste and stir well for 2 minutes. Add the okra, then reduce the heat to low, cover and simmer for about 40 minutes, until the potato is tender.

Scatter over the chopped herbs and crumbled feta (if desired), and serve with crusty bread on the side for mopping up the sauce.

Tip

You can also add chicken to this dish to make it a more substantial meal. Simply brown a few chicken drumsticks for about 10 minutes at the start of cooking, then add them with the okra before simmering.

Natasha Georgopoulos,
Victoria

Yemista

Roasted stuffed vegetables

This is one of my favourite dishes from my yiayia; it takes me back to my childhood, eating her delicious food with my family. Over the past few years I've spent time learning how to cook my yiayia's traditional dishes, creating my own 'Yiayia cookbook' so I can share her recipes with my own family and pass them down through the generations.

SERVES 6–8

3 tablespoons olive oil,
  plus extra for drizzling
1 large onion, chopped
3 spring onions, chopped
1–2 garlic cloves, minced
½ bunch of flat-leaf parsley,
  chopped
2 thyme sprigs, leaves picked
1 tablespoon dried mint
440 g (2 cups) short-grain
  or arborio rice
½–1 teaspoon ground paprika
salt and black pepper
400 g can diced tomatoes
½ teaspoon sugar
6–8 large capsicums
  or tomatoes
1–2 potatoes, cut into bite-
  sized pieces (optional)
lemon wedges, to serve
  (optional)
Greek yoghurt, to serve
  (optional)

Preheat the oven to 200°C (180°C fan-forced).

Heat the oil in a saucepan over medium heat. Add the onion, spring onion and garlic and cook for 5 minutes or until soft and translucent. Stir through the parsley, thyme leaves and mint, then add the rice and paprika and season with salt and pepper to taste. Stir well to combine, then add the diced tomatoes, sugar and 625 ml (2½ cups) of water. Reduce the heat to low and cook, stirring frequently, for 15 minutes or until the rice is almost cooked, but still with some bite. Remove from the heat.

Meanwhile, prepare the capsicums or tomatoes. Slice off the tops, reserving the lids, then carefully remove the seeds and membranes or tomato flesh without piercing the skin. If using tomatoes, you can add the scooped-out flesh to the filling.

Fill the hollowed-out capsicums or tomatoes with the filling and cover with the lids. Transfer to a baking dish and add the potato (if using) to the base of the dish, along with any leftover stuffing. Season with salt and pepper to taste and drizzle with olive oil, then cover tightly with foil. Transfer to the oven and bake for 1¼–1½ hours. Check after 30 minutes of cooking and, if the vegetables look dry, add 125 ml (½ cup) of water to the dish. Remove the foil and continue to bake for another 30 minutes or until the vegetables are golden brown.

Divide the stuffed vegetables among plates, remove the lids and serve with lemon wedges and Greek yoghurt on the side, if desired.

Yemista tis Yiayia

Yiayia's roasted stuffed capsicums

Yiayia makes this traditional Greek dish for herself and Pappou every week. It makes a lovely, light midweek meal that is full of flavour. Taste it and you will see why Yiayia and Pappou love it so much.

SERVES 4

400 g (2 cups) medium-grain rice
boiling water, to cover
3 tablespoons canola oil
1 large onion, diced
500 g mince (half beef topside, half pork fillet, minced twice; ask your butcher to do this for you)
2 teaspoons ground paprika
1 teaspoon salt
1 teaspoon dried oregano
2 tablespoons chopped flat-leaf parsley
8 large red or green capsicums
625 ml (2½ cups) boiling water

Preheat the oven to 220°C (200°C fan-forced).

Pour the rice into a saucepan, cover with boiling water, then place over medium heat and simmer for 5 minutes. Drain and set aside.

Heat the oil in a large frying pan over medium heat, add the onion and cook for 5 minutes or until soft and translucent. Increase the heat to medium–high, then add the mince and cook, breaking up any lumps with the back of a wooden spoon, for 7 minutes or until browned. Stir through the par-cooked rice, paprika, salt, oregano and parsley, then remove from the heat and set aside to cool.

To prepare the capsicums, working with one capsicum at a time, push down on the stalk, then pull up to remove the stalk and core in one swift action. Spoon the mince mixture evenly into the hollowed-out capsicums, then transfer to a roasting tin, making sure the capsicums are standing upright. Divide 250 ml (1 cup) of boiling water among the stuffed capsicums, then pour 375 ml (1½ cups) of boiling water into the base of the tin. Transfer to the oven and roast for 50–60 minutes, covering with foil if the tops start to burn, until the capsicums are soft and cooked through.

Fasolakia

Green beans

This is a time when Yiayia and Pappou unite in the kitchen. It's Pappou's job to remove the pointy ends from the green beans and break them in half. It is all done by hand (no chopping for Pappou).

SERVES 4

400 g green beans
3 tablespoons canola oil
1 large onion, diced
1 teaspoon salt
1 teaspoon ground paprika
1 litre boiling water
crusty bread, to serve

Remove the pointy ends from the green beans and break them in half if they're very long.

Heat the oil in a frying pan with a lid over high heat. Add the onion and cook for 3–4 minutes, until starting to brown. Stir through the salt and paprika, then add the boiling water and the beans. Bring to the boil, then reduce the heat to medium, cover and cook for 10 minutes or until the beans are soft. Drain.

Serve the beans with crusty bread to mop up the juices.

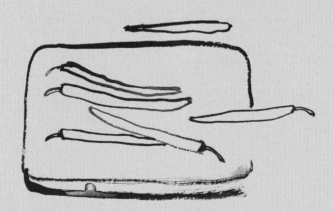

Steph Tsimbourlas,
New South Wales

Fassas fasolia sto fourno

Fassas family's baked beans

I've always known that in Greek culture love is expressed through food. When I was younger, my yiayia Vasiliki Fassas would call me the day before I visited and ask what I wanted her to cook. I would rattle off a list of food: bread, beans, soup, rice, meatballs ... and all of it would be hot and ready when I arrived the next day for lunch, along with a mountain of Tupperware in which to take the food home and eat throughout the week.

As I got older and started cooking for myself, I realised how much labour was involved in making all that food. Yiayia would wake up at 4 am just to prepare it all for me.

Another thing I realised as I got older was that food not only represented love, but our history. This realisation struck in 2016 when my yiayia had two severe strokes. She was in a coma for two weeks, and the first thing that popped into my mind was that I'd never taste her food again; no one could cook Yiayia's dishes! So I sat by her hospital bed every day, begging her to wake up and telling her I was hungry (hoping that this would shock her awake; yiayias hate a hungry grandchild!). I promised myself that when she woke, I would learn her recipes and record all her sacred knowledge.

After two weeks she slowly woke up from her coma. I have never seen so much strength from one person. She spent many months learning to talk, walk and use her hands all over again. In hospital I would ask her every day what ingredients she used in certain dishes, then, as her brain function improved, I would ask her for instructions on how to make them. Eventually she came home, and I would cook as she sat next to me telling me what to do. Fast forward to the past two years, and she has started cooking again while I stand next to her and assist. When she cooks she forgets she's sick – her hands move like they used to, she stands and stirs pots for hours and wants to make extra food so I can take it home. Cooking has been our biggest bond and has helped her heal.

I recently started documenting the recipes, recording videos and photographs as part of a long personal project I'm working on. These recipes not only share instructions, but also stories and histories about my ancestors and family that would otherwise be forgotten.

SERVES 6–8

500 g dried large white beans,
   such as great northern beans,
   soaked overnight in cold water
extra-virgin olive oil
3 large onions, thickly sliced
   (plus 1 extra for Maria;
   see Note)
salt and black pepper
2 teaspoons ground paprika,
   plus extra if desired
handful of dried mint, plus
   extra to serve (optional)
7–10 mint sprigs
500 g passata

To serve

fresh bread or toast
crumbled feta
black olives

Drain the beans, then transfer to a large stockpot and cover with 4 litres of water. Bring to the boil over high heat, then reduce the heat to a simmer and cook for 25–30 minutes or until soft, but still with some bite. My pappou recommends adding a glug of olive oil and a large pinch of paprika to the water while the beans cook to give them extra flavour, but you don't have to do this.

Meanwhile, preheat the oven to 180°C (160°C fan-forced).

Heat a generous glug of olive oil in a large frying pan over low heat. Add the onion, season with 2 large pinches of salt and pepper and 2 teaspoons of paprika and gently cook for 20–30 minutes, until the onion is soft and sweet. (If you're starting to get hungry and can't resist the smell of cooking onions, use the extra onion to make yourself a 'Maria sandwich'; see Note.)

Transfer the beans, together with 375 ml (1½ cups) of their cooking liquid, to a large baking dish. Add the cooked onion, dried and fresh mint, passata and 3 tablespoons of olive oil. Season with salt and pepper to taste and use a spoon to swirl the ingredients until well combined. Transfer the dish to the oven and cook for 15 minutes or until a slight crust forms on the surface. Remove the beans from the oven and stir well, then reduce the heat to 160°C (140°C fan-forced) and cook for a further 10 minutes, stirring the beans from time to time, until most of the liquid is absorbed. Increase the heat to 180°C (160°C fan-forced) again and cook for 10–15 minutes or until the beans are soft and juicy and a crust has formed on the top again.

You can stir in some extra dried mint before serving if you like. Eat the beans with fresh bread or toast, with feta and olives on the side – it makes the perfect breakfast! Yiayia used to make three large dishes for the whole family to freeze and eat throughout the month – it was the best surprise to find a hidden container in the freezer. See overleaf for the finished dish.

Note

While cooking beans for the first time with Yiayia, she told me about her sister, Maria, who could never wait for them to finish cooking. She would always fry an extra onion and then eat it on bread while the beans cooked (it's delicious). Yiayia loved that I embraced Maria's style and made sure the extra onion was added to this recipe when I wrote it down. 'One extra onion for Maria,' she said.

Fassas fasolia sto fourno (Fassas family's baked beans), see page 162

Fried feta,
Yiayia style

Cut 200 g of firm feta into
4 cm × 3 cm rectangles, about
1.5 cm thick. Place a little plain
flour on a plate and dust the feta
in the flour. Heat 80 ml (⅓ cup) of
canola oil in a non-stick frying pan
over high heat. Add the floured feta
and cook for 20 seconds on each
side until golden brown. Transfer
to a plate and serve.

Glika

Sweets

Zak Antoniou,
South Australia

Koulourakia

Greek Easter biscuits

This recipe means so much to me as I no longer have my yiayia around, but every time I eat
these biscuits it reminds me of her and, of course, my pappou. As a kid, I never really ate store-
bought biscuits. My yiayia would make these koulourakia, along with other Greek biscuits,
all year round and they were a staple in her pantry.

To this day, my mum still makes Greek Easter biscuits and they are a treat served with coffee
in the morning, or as my pappou would eat them: crushed up in a bowl with warm water.
It was the Greek version of Weet-Bix!

MAKES ABOUT 20

125 g unsalted butter,
   at room temperature
165 g (¾ cup) caster sugar
3 large eggs
1½ tablespoons full-cream milk
2 teaspoons vanilla sugar
500 g (3⅓ cups) self-raising
   flour, plus extra if needed
sesame seeds, for sprinkling
   (optional)

Preheat the oven to 180°C (160°C fan-forced). Line a baking tray
with baking paper.

Place the butter and caster sugar in the bowl of a stand mixer
fitted with the paddle attachment. Beat on high speed for
4–5 minutes, until light and fluffy. Add two of the eggs, one at
a time, and beat until well combined, then, with the mixer
running, slowly pour in the milk and add the vanilla sugar.
Gradually add the flour 150 g (1 cup) at a time and beat until the
dough comes away from the side of the bowl. The dough should
be soft and not sticky – if it is, add a little more flour and continue
to mix.

Take 1½ tablespoons of dough and roll it into a long thin rope.
From here, you can make any shape you like, but the traditional
shape is a twisted braid with a loop at the top.

Transfer to the prepared tray, then repeat with the remaining
dough to make about 20 biscuits, leaving enough space between
each biscuit to rise.

Lightly beat the remaining egg, then brush the top of each biscuit
to glaze. Sprinkle over some sesame seeds, if you like.

Bake for 15–20 minutes, until light golden. Transfer to a wire rack
to cool, then store in an airtight container for up to 3 weeks.

Kourabiethes

Shortbread 'moon' biscuits

Everyone loves Yiayia's moon biscuits! Buttery and soft and with a hint of anise from the ouzo, they are the perfect sweet treat to serve with strong coffee.

MAKES 25

250 g unsalted butter, at room
temperature
160 g (1 cup) pure icing sugar,
plus extra for coating
1 teaspoon vanilla sugar
2 egg yolks, lightly beaten
525 g (3½ cups) self-raising
flour, plus extra if needed
and for dusting
25 ml ouzo

Preheat the oven to 170°C (150°C fan-forced). Grease a large baking tray.

Cream the butter, icing sugar and vanilla sugar together in a large bowl until smooth. Add the egg and mix until combined, then stir in the flour. Add the ouzo and mix well, then, using your hands, knead the dough in the bowl until smooth, adding a little more flour if the dough is still sticky.

Lightly flour a work surface. Grab a handful of dough and press it into a 2 cm thick disc. Using a small coffee cup or 6 cm round cookie cutter, cut out half-moon shapes, then use your hands to gently flatten them to about 1 cm thick. Repeat with the remaining dough until you have 25 biscuits.

Transfer the biscuits to the prepared tray and bake for 30 minutes or until golden brown. Set aside to cool for 10 minutes, then dip the biscuits in icing sugar to completely coat.

Serve with coffee.

Leftover moon biscuits will keep in an airtight container in the pantry for 5 days.

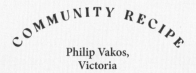

Philip Vakos,
Victoria

Rizogalo me raventi

Rice pudding with rhubarb

Growing up, rizogalo was a staple snack readily available in my yiayia's fridge. She would whip it out often, but if I'm honest it was never my favourite dessert. As I grew older, however, I really started to appreciate the simplicity and deliciousness of it ... much to Yiayia's delight. I often serve rizogalo at my restaurant, but I've made a few tweaks by folding cardamom cream through the rice pudding and topping it with rhubarb and berries. It really elevates it to another level. So here is my yiayia's rizogalo ... with my own little twist. Enjoy!

SERVES 4

110 g (½ cup) arborio rice
500 ml (2 cups) full-cream milk
1 vanilla bean, split lengthways
100 g caster sugar, plus extra
    if desired
60 g unsalted butter
1 bunch of rhubarb, stalks
    trimmed and cut into
    7 cm lengths
1 teaspoon ground cardamom
250 ml (1 cup) thickened cream
blackberries or halved
    strawberries, to serve

Rinse the rice under cold running water until the water runs clear. Transfer to a saucepan and add the milk and vanilla bean. Place over low heat and simmer, stirring frequently, for 20 minutes or until the rice is tender. Remove from the heat and add 80 g (⅓ cup) of the sugar, then stir through until the sugar is dissolved. Set aside to cool a little.

Meanwhile, to prepare the rhubarb, melt the butter in a saucepan over medium heat. Add the rhubarb and cook, stirring frequently, for 10–15 minutes, until tender. Add the remaining sugar and stir until dissolved, then set aside.

In another bowl, whisk together the cardamom and cream until soft peaks form. You can whisk some sugar through the cream if you prefer it sweeter.

Remove the vanilla bean from the cooled rice mixture and discard, then gently fold the cardamom cream through the rice mixture to lighten it.

Divide the rice pudding among bowls. Serve warm, topped with the rhubarb and some fresh blackberries or strawberries, drizzled with the leftover rhubarb syrup in the pan.

Horyiatikos halvas

Village-style halva

Halva is a classic Greek dish. It was traditionally made at the end of the wheat harvest in Yiayia's village. It uses very few ingredients, but is delicious nonetheless. Enjoy with a cup of tea.

MAKES 12

160 g (1 cup) fine semolina
100 ml canola oil
235 g sugar
500 ml (2 cups) boiling water

Place the semolina and oil in a large frying pan over medium heat. Cook, stirring constantly, for 8 minutes or until the semolina is toasted and golden, then remove from the heat.

Combine the sugar and boiling water in a heatproof bowl and stir until the sugar is dissolved. Add half the sugar water to the toasted semolina and place over low heat. Cook for 1 minute, then add the remaining sugar water and stir until completely combined.

Transfer the halva to a flat plate then, when cool enough to handle, scoop a heaped tablespoon of the mixture into your hand and mould into an oval shape. Set aside and repeat with the remaining halva to make 12 pieces.

The halva will keep in an airtight container in the fridge or pantry for up to 1 week.

Creme caramel

My yiayia used to make this dish whenever we had functions or family get-togethers – everyone loved her creme caramel, and I know Daniel and Luke's mother, Teresa, would have enjoyed this on at least one of these occasions. Each time I see a creme caramel, it reminds me of my yiayia. She made sure she passed this recipe on to all of us because, in her words, 'it's the best creme caramel recipe!' She was right.

SERVES 12

2 tablespoons sugar
1 litre full-cream milk
4 eggs
2 teaspoons vanilla paste
395 g can sweetened
   condensed milk

Preheat the oven to 180°C (160°C fan-forced).

Place the sugar and 2 tablespoons of water in a small saucepan. Cook over low heat for about 5 minutes, until bubbling and dark golden brown, then carefully pour into a 22 cm round cake tin and swirl to coat the base. Set aside to cool.

Gently heat the milk in a saucepan over medium heat until warmed through.

In a bowl, whisk the eggs until lightly beaten, then add the vanilla paste and condensed milk and whisk well. Whisking constantly, slowly add the warm milk until combined.

Pour the custard over the cooled caramel and let it sit for a couple of minutes to allow any bubbles to settle. Place the tin in a larger roasting tin and half-fill the roasting tin with water to make a water bath. Bake for 1½ hours, then carefully jiggle the cake tin to see if the custard is set. If it is still watery, continue to cook for another 30 minutes or until the custard is firm to touch. Cover the top with foil if the custard is browning too quickly.

Leave the creme caramel in the oven to cool completely, then place in the fridge until ready to serve.

To remove the creme caramel from the tin, run a knife around the edge of the tin, then place a plate on top and invert the creme caramel onto the plate. Cut into pieces and serve.

Lagithes

Greek doughnuts

With a soft, gooey centre and a crunchy exterior, these sweet pockets of golden goodness will have you grinning from ear to ear. Yiayia coats her doughnuts in honey before sprinkling them with a little cinnamon. It's impossible to stop at just one!

MAKES ABOUT 16

10 g fresh yeast (see Note) or
   1 teaspoon instant dried yeast
400 ml warm water, plus extra
   if needed
485 g (3¼ cups) plain flour
pinch of salt
1 egg, lightly beaten
neutral oil, such as canola or
   grapeseed, for deep-frying
260 g (¾ cup) honey
ground cinnamon, for sprinkling

Combine the yeast and a little of the warm water in a jug and set aside until starting to bubble slightly.

Sift the flour and salt into a large bowl. Make a well in the centre and add the yeast mixture, egg and remaining warm water. Stir with a spoon, then use your hands to bring the mixture together to form a very thick batter, making sure there are no lumps.

Fill a sink with hot water and place the bowl of dough in the sink. Cover with a plate and stand for 30 minutes or until the dough rises to the top of the bowl and is thick and slightly stretchy.

Heat enough oil for deep-frying in a large heavy-based saucepan over medium–high heat. To test if the oil is hot enough, carefully drop a small piece of dough into the oil; if it sizzles, the oil is ready.

Working in batches, transfer the dough to a piping bag with a plain nozzle and pipe small dollops (about 1½ tablespoons) of the dough into the hot oil (Yiayia uses her hand as a makeshift piping bag, using her thumb to push blobs of dough over her forefinger). Don't overcrowd the pan as the dough will double in size as it cooks. Cook for 5–6 minutes, using a slotted spoon to flip the doughnuts every now and then, until golden brown. Scoop the doughnuts onto paper towel to drain, then repeat with the remaining dough.

Place the honey in a small saucepan and gently warm over low heat until runny. Drizzle the honey over the doughnuts and sprinkle with a little ground cinnamon. Enjoy while warm.

Note

Fresh yeast can be bought from your local bakery, but substitute with instant dried yeast if easier.

Lagithes (Greek doughnuts), see page 178

Val Christodoulou,
Victoria

Karitha & lemoni glíko

Coconut & lemon syrup cake

My mother-in-law gave me this recipe, along with the pan to cook it in (which I still use to this day), 30-odd years ago. It has been a family favourite for years and a winner at most gatherings. I also have fond memories of Daniel and Luke's mother, Teresa, being very partial to this particular cake and that just warms my heart.

SERVES 12

250 g unsalted butter, softened
230 g (1 cup) caster sugar
6 eggs
150 g (1 cup) self-raising
    flour, sifted
1½ teaspoons vanilla sugar
250 g desiccated coconut

Lemon syrup
460 g (2 cups) caster sugar
juice of 3 lemons

Preheat the oven to 180°C (160°C fan-forced). Grease a 24 cm round cake tin (or use a springform tin) with butter.

Place the butter and caster sugar in a bowl and cream together until light and fluffy. Beat in the eggs one at a time, making sure each egg is fully incorporated before adding the next to prevent the mixture curdling.

Gently fold in the sifted flour, vanilla sugar and most of the desiccated coconut, reserving 25 g (¼ cup) to sprinkle on top of the cooked cake. Gently mix until just combined – the batter will be quite thick. Spoon the batter into the prepared cake tin and smooth the surface with a spatula.

Bake for 30–35 minutes, until the top is golden and a skewer inserted into the middle of the cake comes out clean.

While the cake is cooking, make the lemon syrup. Place the sugar, lemon juice and 750 ml (3 cups) of water in a large saucepan and bring to the boil over medium heat. Gently boil for 15 minutes, then set aside to cool slightly.

Let the cake cool in the tin for 10 minutes, then turn out onto a wire rack and place a plate underneath. Gradually pour the warm syrup over the cake, allowing it to completely soak in, then decorate with the remaining desiccated coconut.

Transfer the cake to the plate, then slice and serve. It is lovely served warm but will also stay nice and moist, thanks to the syrup, for up to 1 week in an airtight container.

Revani

Semolina tray cake

Revani is a semolina tray cake soaked in sugar syrup, popular throughout Greece and Turkey. In Yiayia's home village, the cake was reserved for festivals and special occasions. It is delightfully sweet, with a soft crumbly texture from the semolina. It is also very easy to make!

SERVES 15

160 g (1 cup) fine semolina
75 g (½ cup) self-raising flour
6 eggs, lightly beaten
230 g (1 cup) caster sugar
1 teaspoon baking powder
1 teaspoon vanilla sugar

Sugar syrup
460 g (2 cups) caster sugar
500 ml (2 cups) boiling water

Preheat the oven to 180°C (160°C fan-forced). Lightly grease a 30 cm × 20 cm cake tin.

Combine the semolina and flour in a large bowl. Add the beaten egg, caster sugar, baking powder and vanilla sugar and mix until smooth.

Pour the batter into the prepared tin and cook for 15–20 minutes, until the top is golden and a skewer inserted into the middle of the cake comes out clean. Remove from the oven and set aside to cool for 15 minutes.

Meanwhile, to make the sugar syrup, combine the sugar and boiling water in a saucepan and stir until the sugar is dissolved. Pour the syrup over the cake and let it soak in for 20 minutes or until fully absorbed.

Cut into squares and serve. Any leftover cake will keep in an airtight container for 3 days.

Angie Triantos,
Victoria

Galopita

Greek custard pie

This is a sweet dish that my yiayia used to make for every special family function.
We now make it in her absence to feel close to her – it's simple and quick to make.

I wish I had taken more time when she was alive to learn both her sweet and savoury recipes;
her love for food and her way around the kitchen was truly special and something we always
took for granted. No one cooks like Yiayia. I can't wait to try my hand at making the recipes
featured in this book!

SERVES 10–12

1 litre full-cream milk
230 g (1 cup) caster sugar
160 g (1 cup) fine semolina
1 teaspoon lemon zest
25 g vanilla sugar
pinch of salt
75 g unsalted butter
5 eggs, lightly beaten
ground cinnamon, for sprinkling

Preheat the oven to 180°C (160°C fan-forced).

Place the milk, caster sugar, semolina, lemon zest, vanilla sugar, salt and 50 g of the butter in a saucepan and set over high heat. Whisking constantly, heat the mixture for 3–5 minutes, until thickened. Reduce the heat to medium–low, add the eggs and stir until well combined. Remove from the heat.

Place the remaining butter in a 25 cm square baking dish, then pop it in the oven to melt. Once melted, pour the custard into the dish – the custard will push the melted butter up the sides. Use a spatula to spread the butter over the top of the custard. Transfer to the oven and bake for 30–40 minutes, until just set.

Sprinkle a little ground cinnamon over the top of the custard, then allow the custard to cool and set for 15 minutes before cutting into 5 cm squares.

Eat warm or keep in an airtight container in the fridge for up to 4 days.

Village-style baklava

When Yiayia's mother visited Australia, she taught her daughter this simple baklava recipe from their village back home. Yiayia still makes it to this day. It holds a special place in her heart.

MAKES ABOUT 22

200 g (2 cups) walnuts, plus extra, finely chopped, for sprinkling
375 g packet of frozen filo pastry, thawed
125 ml (½ cup) canola oil
460 g (2 cups) caster sugar

Blend, process or chop the walnuts until finely chopped (Yiayia uses a mouli grater).

Preheat the oven to 200°C (180°C fan-forced).

Working with one sheet of filo pastry at a time, and keeping the rest covered under a damp tea towel while you work, gently brush a little oil and sprinkle 1 tablespoon of finely chopped walnuts over the pastry. Starting at the edge closest to you, concertina the pastry sheet into a long strip. Bend the top third of the strip to the right and the bottom third of the strip to the left, to create an 'S' shape. Repeat with the remaining pastry, most of the oil and all the walnuts. Transfer to a baking tray and brush the remaining oil over the folded pastry.

Transfer to the oven and bake for 10 minutes, at which point the tops should be golden brown. Turn the baklava over and cook for another 5 minutes or until both sides are golden.

Meanwhile, place the sugar and 500 ml (2 cups) of water in a saucepan over medium–low heat. Cook for 5–6 minutes, until the sugar is dissolved and you have a light syrup. Set aside to cool for 8 minutes.

While still warm, dip each baklava into the sugar syrup to completely coat, then transfer to a serving plate. Sprinkle with extra chopped walnuts and serve.

Note

For extra yumminess, drizzle honey over the baklava and serve with vanilla ice cream.

Christina Panagopoulos,
South Australia

Galaktoboureko

Filo custard pie with lemon–honey syrup

After I got married, I sought out Greek recipes reminiscent of my mother's cooking. I started a page on Instagram called Pieces of Greece, where I share Greek recipes and inspiration. This galaktoboureko recipe is dear to my heart. It was given to me by my mother, and it evolved to become my own. A bit more of this, a little less of that. Thank you to my mum, Yiannoula. This filo custard pie was my first introduction to Greek cooking.

SERVES 16

6 egg yolks, at room
  temperature
230 g (1 cup) caster sugar
1.5 litres full-cream milk
160 g (1 cup) fine semolina
1 teaspoon vanilla essence
1 tablespoon vanilla sugar
zest of ¼ lemon
150 g unsalted butter
375 g packet of frozen filo
  pastry, thawed

Lemon–honey syrup

230 g (1 cup) caster sugar
rind of ½ lemon
1 tablespoon honey

First prepare the lemon–honey syrup, as it must be at room temperature when the pie comes out of the oven. Place the sugar, lemon rind and 185 ml (¾ cup) of water in a small saucepan. Bring to the boil over high heat, stirring once. Reduce the heat to medium and simmer for 7 minutes, then stir in the honey. Set aside to cool completely.

Preheat the oven to 190°C (170°C fan-forced).

To make the custard, ensure you have all the ingredients measured out and ready to go, as once you start whisking you can't stop.

Place the egg yolks and caster sugar in the bowl of a stand mixer with the whisk attached and whisk on medium speed for 6–7 minutes, until the sugar has dissolved and the mixture is pale and fluffy.

Combine the milk and semolina in a large saucepan and place over medium heat. Whisk constantly for 5 minutes until just warm (not hot), pale and frothy. Still whisking constantly, add the egg yolk mixture, vanilla essence, vanilla sugar and lemon zest, then whisk for 10–12 minutes, until the mixture is pale and thick. Add 50 g of the butter and whisk for another minute until melted. The custard should be thick and glossy.

Butter a 25 cm × 30 cm baking dish. Melt the remaining butter in a small saucepan over medium heat.

Lay the filo pastry on a work surface, covered with baking paper and a clean damp tea towel. Take two sheets of filo and line the base of the baking dish, then brush all over with the melted butter. Repeat this layering, using two sheets of filo at a time and brushing with butter, until you've used half the filo sheets. Pour in the custard, then top with the remaining filo and melted butter until you've used all the ingredients. Ensure that the top layer of

Glika

pastry looks neat, trimming any excess edges, then use a spatula to gently tuck in the edges to form a crust.

Using a sharp knife, score the top layers of filo pastry into diamonds. Transfer to the oven and bake for 45–50 minutes, until the pastry is light golden brown .

Allow the pie to cool for 1 minute, then ladle over the lemon–honey syrup (discard the lemon rind). Set aside to cool and set for at least 2 hours before cutting and serving. See overleaf for the finished dish.

Any leftover custard pie will keep in an airtight container in the pantry for 2 days or in an airtight container in the fridge for up to 1 week. It is best served at room temperature.

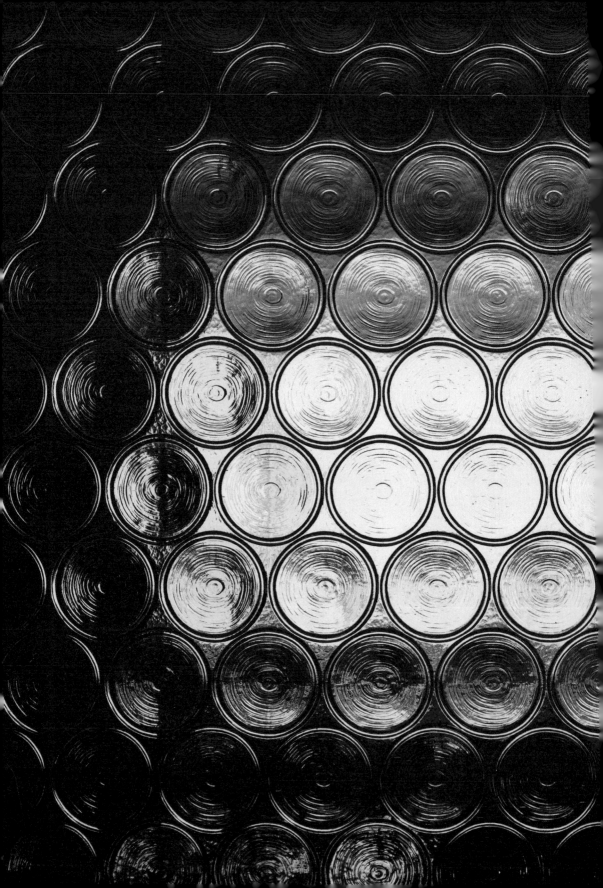

Galaktoboureko (filo custard pie with lemon–honey syrup), see page 192

Connie Siopoulos,
South Australia

Portokalopita

Orange syrup cake

I remember staying in Greece one year with my relatives, and we were invited to someone's house for dinner at the last minute. My yiayia started running around frantically as she didn't have much time to make something for dessert. She found filo pastry in the fridge and whipped this up.

SERVES 12

375 g packet of frozen filo pastry, thawed
5 large oranges
5 eggs
200 g Greek yoghurt
185 ml (¾ cup) olive oil
115 g (½ cup) caster sugar
1 tablespoon baking powder
1 teaspoon vanilla essence

Orange syrup

460 g (2 cups) caster sugar
1 cinnamon stick
1 orange, halved

Start by making the orange syrup. Place the sugar, cinnamon and 375 ml (1½ cups) of water in a saucepan over medium–high heat. Squeeze in the orange juice and add the squeezed halves, then bring to the boil and boil vigorously for 10 minutes. Remove from the heat and strain into a bowl (discard the orange halves and cinnamon stick). Set aside to cool while you prepare the cake.

Preheat the oven to 120°C (100°C fan-forced).

Working with one sheet at a time, scrunch up the filo pastry, then arrange the bunches on a baking tray in a single layer (you'll need more than one tray; no need to grease or line them). Bake for about 15 minutes, then turn over and bake for a further 15 minutes until crisp and light golden.

When cool enough to handle, use your hands to crush the filo sheets into a large bowl.

Increase the oven temperature to 195°C (175°C fan-forced). Lightly grease a 22 cm × 33 cm roasting tin.

Zest and juice three of the oranges. Combine the orange zest and juice, eggs, yoghurt, olive oil, sugar, baking powder and vanilla essence in the bowl of a stand mixer with the paddle attached. Mix on high speed for about 2 minutes, until light and fluffy. Pour the batter over the crushed filo and gently stir to combine. Transfer to the prepared tin.

Finely slice the remaining orange into half moons and decorate the top of the cake in rows. Transfer to the oven and bake for 45–50 minutes, until the top is golden and a skewer inserted into the middle of the cake comes out clean.

Remove the cake from the oven and immediately pour the cooled syrup over the hot cake (it is important that the syrup is cool and the cake is hot). Set aside for an hour to cool, then slice into 12 pieces and serve. Any leftover cake will keep in an airtight container in the fridge for 3 days.

Conversion charts

Measuring cups and spoons may vary slightly from one country to another, but the difference is generally not enough to affect a recipe. All cup and spoon measures are level. One Australian metric measuring cup holds 250 ml (8 fl oz), one Australian metric tablespoon holds 20 ml (4 teaspoons) and one Australian metric teaspoon holds 5 ml. North America, New Zealand and the UK use a 15 ml (3-teaspoon) tablespoon.

LENGTH

METRIC	IMPERIAL
3 mm	⅛ inch
6 mm	¼ inch
1 cm	½ inch
2.5 cm	1 inch
5 cm	2 inches
18 cm	7 inches
20 cm	8 inches
23 cm	9 inches
25 cm	10 inches
30 cm	12 inches

LIQUID MEASURES

ONE AMERICAN PINT	ONE IMPERIAL PINT
500 ml (16 fl oz)	600 ml (20 fl oz)

CUP	METRIC	IMPERIAL
⅛ cup	30 ml	1 fl oz
¼ cup	60 ml	2 fl oz
⅓ cup	80 ml	2½ fl oz
½ cup	125 ml	4 fl oz
⅔ cup	160 ml	5 fl oz
¾ cup	180 ml	6 fl oz
1 cup	250 ml	8 fl oz
2 cups	500 ml	16 fl oz
2¼ cups	560 ml	20 fl oz
4 cups	1 litre	32 fl oz

DRY MEASURES

The most accurate way to measure dry ingredients is to weigh them. However, if using a cup, add the ingredient loosely to the cup and level with a knife; don't compact the ingredient unless the recipe requests 'firmly packed'.

METRIC	IMPERIAL
15 g	½ oz
30 g	1 oz
60 g	2 oz
125 g	4 oz (¼ lb)
185 g	6 oz
250 g	8 oz (½ lb)
375 g	12 oz (¾ lb)
500 g	16 oz (1 lb)
1 kg	32 oz (2 lb)

OVEN TEMPERATURES

CELSIUS	FAHRENHEIT
100°C	200°F
120°C	250°F
150°C	300°F
160°C	325°F
180°C	350°F
200°C	400°F
220°C	425°F

OVEN TEMPERATURES

CELSIUS	GAS MARK
110°C	¼
130°C	½
140°C	1
150°C	2
170°C	3
180°C	4
190°C	5
200°C	6
220°C	7
230°C	8
240°C	9
250°C	10

Thanks

Thank you to everyone who has supported us on our journey, and to our Yiayia Next Door social media community – you have made this happen. While creating this cookbook we laughed, cried and ate (oh, did we eat), but we couldn't have brought it all to life without a few special people.

To our neighbours, Yiayia, Pappou, Helen, Fay, Nick and Tex, thank you for the many years of friendship between our families, for supporting us through our hardest time and for making sure that we're always well fed.

To our wonderful family, Nonna Rosa Mancuso, Franca Mancuso, Nick Franco, Catherine Franco, Nicholas Franco, Patrick Mancuso, Leilani Buck, Velvet Mancuso, Rosina Mancuso, Melina Mancuso, Giuseppe Mercatante, Alessia Mercatante, Mattia Campaiola, Mariellen Siopoulos, Maja Gasiorek, Marlowe and Wags, thank you for all that you have done for us. You have supported and nurtured us, and always made sure that we had a place to call home (even when we both felt lost). To our nonno, Giovanni Mancuso, your morals and way of life have been instilled in all of us.

Thank you to the Plum and Pan Macmillan team: Mary Small, Publisher; Clare Marshall, Project Editor; Lucy Heaver, Editor; Andrea McNamara, Publishing Consultant; Daniel New, Designer and Illustrator; Mark Roper, Photographer; Lee Blaylock, Stylist; Caroline Griffiths, Chef; and Gemma Smith, Chef. You gave us the opportunity to create something special and pay tribute to our beautiful mother. You made this all happen and brought our vision to life. Thank you for all your hard work.

Thanks to our very own Yiayia Next Door team: Tom Cowie, Journalist; Ryan Sauer, Videographer; Daniel DeSilva, Videographer; Sanna Conquest, Advisor; Frank Hinoporos, Legal Advisor; and Connie Siopoulos, Translator. We are so grateful for the hours you have spent, from the very beginning, working with us to create and build Yiayia Next Door.

Thank you to all the recipe contributors from the Yiayia Next Door social media community: Zak Antoniou, Kelly Ardonis, Helen Bouzis, Val Christodoulou, Natasha Georgopoulos, Nicholas Giakoumelos, Tania Gogos Wilson, Mary Kalifatidis, Zoe Konikkos, Kathy Marin, Katherine Nikolakoudis, Elle Nikolaou-Abdo, Christina Panagopoulos, Tina Roukis, Connie Siopoulos, Angie Triantos, Steph Tsimbourlas, Philip Vakos, Crystal Marie Vicario, and Debbie Xanthopoulos. Thank you for taking the time to submit these incredible recipes and family stories. We are honoured to share them.

We extend our thanks to Paola Piccione, Tony Harwood, Andrew Tinney, Kylie Duthie, Salva Pusello, the Christodoulou family, the Petovic family and the Baullo family, who have supported us throughout our lives, and to all our friends who we call family (you know who you are).

And finally, to our mum, Teresa Mancuso, you will always be our inspiration.

Index

A

Anne's Greek Easter bread 74–5
artichokes: Chicken & artichoke fricassee 106–7
avgolemono, Eftichia's 61
avgolemono, Giakoumelos family's 62

B

Baked fish parcels 102
Baked fish with onion & potato 105
Baked rice with mince 92
baklava, Village-style 190
Bamies 157
Bean soup 56
beans
    Bean soup 56
    Beef, bean & potato stew 112
    Fassas family's baked beans 162–3
    Green beans 161
bechamel, halloumi 95
bechamel, traditional 119
beef
    Baked rice with mince 92
    Beef, bean & potato stew 112
    Cabbage rolls 125
    Cypriot-style pastitsio 94–5
    Greek-style ragu 131
    Katina's moussaka 118–19
    Lasagne 91
    Meatball soup 65
    meatballs 65
    Meatballs 116
    Mince & leek filo pie 46
    Pasta squares with meatballs 86
    Yiayia's roasted stuffed capsicums 160
Beef, bean & potato stew 112
biscuits
    Greek Easter biscuits 171
    Shortbread 'moon' biscuits 172
bread
    Anne's Greek Easter bread 74–5
    Debbie's Greek Easter bread 78–9

    Fried bread with feta 73
    Homemade bread 68
brine, pickling 146
bullhorn peppers see capsicum

C

cabbage
    Cabbage & pork stew 115
    Cabbage rolls 125
    Pickled vegetables 146
Cabbage & pork stew 115
Cabbage rolls 125
cakes
    Coconut & lemon syrup cake 183
    Orange syrup cake 197
    Semolina tray cake 186
capsicum
    Baked fish parcels 102
    Baked rice with mince 92
    Bean soup 56
    Beef, bean & potato stew 112
    Dried red pepper mash 148
    drying 148
    Fried peppers with scrambled eggs 24
    Garden salad, Yiayia style 142
    Grilled peppers 138
    Lentil soup 58
    Pickled vegetables 146
    Red rice with chicken & spinach 82
    Roasted stuffed vegetables 158
    Yiayia's roasted stuffed capsicums 160
carrots
    Giakoumelos family's avgolemono 62
    Katina's moussaka 118–19
casserole, Okra, tomato & potato 157
celery
    Eftichia's avgolemono 61
    Giakoumelos family's avgolemono 62
    Katina's moussaka 118–19
cheese
    Cypriot-style pastitsio 94–5

halloumi bechamel 95
Katina's moussaka 118–19
Lasagne 91
Mum's cannelloni 97
traditional bechamel 119
see also feta, ricotta
Cheese pie 42
chicken
    Chicken & artichoke fricassee 106–7
    Chicken & rice 108
    Chicken livers 113
    Chicken noodle soup 63
    Eftichia's avgolemono 61
    Giakoumelos family's avgolemono 62
    Okra, tomato & potato casserole 157
    Red rice with chicken & spinach 82
Chicken & artichoke fricassee 106–7
Chicken & rice 108
Chicken livers 113
Chicken noodle soup 63
chillies
    Cabbage & pork stew 115
    Dried red pepper mash 148
    preserving 89
Coconut & lemon syrup cake 183
Creme caramel 177
cucumber
    Garden salad, Yiayia style 142
    growing tips 151
custard pie, Filo, with lemon–honey syrup 192–3
custard pie, Greek 189
Cypriot-style pastitsio 94–5

D
Debbie's Greek Easter bread 78–9
dough, spanakopita 38
doughnuts, Greek 178
Dried red pepper mash 148

E
Eftichia's avgolemono 61
eggplant: Katina's moussaka 118–19
eggs
Chicken & artichoke fricassee 106–7
    Chicken noodle soup 63
    Coconut & lemon syrup cake 183
    Creme caramel 177
    Eftichia's avgolemono 61
    Filo cheese pie 48–9
    Filo custard pie with lemon–honey
      syrup 192–3
    Fried egg, Yiayia style 26
    Fried peppers with scrambled eggs 24
    Giakoumelos family's avgolemono 62
    Greek custard pie 189
    Greek Easter biscuits 171
    Meatball soup 65

Orange syrup cake 197
Scrambled eggs with spinach 29
Scrambled eggs, Yiayia style 32
Semolina tray cake 186
Shortbread 'moon' biscuits 172
Yiayia's egg & feta filo pie 47

F
Fakes 58
Fasolada 56
Fasolakia 161
Fassas family's baked beans 162–3
Fassas fasolia sto fourno 162–3
fennel: Chicken & artichoke fricassee 106–7
feta
    Cheese pie 42
    Filo cheese pie 48–9
    Fried bread with feta 73
    Fried feta, Yiayia style 166
    Scrambled eggs, Yiayia style 32
    Spanakopita 38–9
    Spinach & rice 85
    Yiayia's egg & feta filo pie 47
Filo cheese pie 48–9
Filo custard pie with lemon–honey
  syrup 192–3
fish
    Baked fish parcels 102
    Baked fish with onion & potato 105
Fithosoupa 63
fricassee, Chicken & artichoke 106–7
Fried bread with feta 73
Fried egg, Yiayia style 26
Fried feta, Yiayia style 166
Fried peppers with scrambled eggs 24

G
Galaktoboureko 192–3
Galopita 189
Garden salad, Yiayia style 142
garden tips, Pappou's 150–1
Giakoumelos family's avgolemono 62
Giouvarlakia 65
Greek custard pie 189
Greek doughnuts 178
Greek Easter biscuits 171
Greek-style ragu 131
Green beans 161
Grilled peppers 138

H
halloumi bechamel 95
halva, Village-style 176
Hilopites me keftedakia 86
Homemade bread 68
Horyiatikos halvas 176
Htipito spanaki me avga 29

K
Karitha & lemoni gliko 183
Katina's moussaka 118–19
Keftedes 116
Kokkinisto 131
Kokkino rizi me kotopoulo & spanaki 82
Kotopoulo fricassee me agginares 106–7
Kotopoulo me rizi 108
Koulourakia 171
Kourabiethes 172
Kreatopita me praso 46

L
Lagithes 178
Lahanika toursi 146
Lahano dolmades 125
Lahanohirino stifado 115
lamb
    Greek-style ragu 131
    Marinated lamb cutlets 122
    Mum's rack of lamb with jam 126
Lasagne 91
leeks
    Bean soup 56
    Meatball soup 65
    Mince & leek filo pie 46
Lemon potatoes 145
lemon syrup 183
lemon–honey syrup 192
lemons
    Anne's Greek Easter bread 74–5
    Chicken & artichoke fricassee 106–7
    Coconut & lemon syrup cake 183
    Eftichia's avgolemono 61
    Filo custard pie with lemon–honey syrup 192–3
    Giakoumelos family's avgolemono 62
    Greek custard pie 189
    Lemon potatoes 145
    lemon syrup 183
    lemon–honey syrup 192
    Marinated lamb cutlets 122
    Meatball soup 65
    Mum's rack of lamb with jam 126
Lentil soup 58

M
Makaronia tou fournou 94–5
Marinated lamb cutlets 122
mash, Dried red pepper 148
Meatball soup 65
Meatballs 116
Mince & leek filo pie 46
Mizithra keftedes 22
Moshari me fasolakia 112
moussaka, Katina's 118–19
Mum's cannelloni 97
Mum's rack of lamb with jam 126

N
nuts: Village-style baklava 190

O
Okra, tomato & potato casserole 157
olives, preserving 89
orange syrup 197
Orange syrup cake 197
oranges
    Anne's Greek Easter bread 74–5
    Debbie's Greek Easter bread 78–9
    orange syrup 197
    Orange syrup cake 197
ouzo: Shortbread 'moon' biscuits 172

P
Paidakia tis skaras 122
Pappou's garden tips 150–1
pasta
    Chicken noodle soup 63
    Cypriot-style pastitsio 94–5
    Greek-style ragu 131
    Lasagne 91
    Mum's cannelloni 97
    Pasta squares with meatballs 86
Pasta squares with meatballs 86
Patates lemonates 145
Pickled vegetables 146
pickling brine 146
pies
    Cheese pie 42
    Filo cheese pie 48–9
    Filo custard pie with lemon–honey syrup 192–3
    Greek custard pie 189
    Mince & leek filo pie 46
    Spanakopita 38–9
    Yiayia's egg & feta filo pie 47
Pilafi me kima 92
Piperies tis skaras 138
pork
    Baked rice with mince 92
    Cabbage & pork stew 115
    Cabbage rolls 125
    Cypriot-style pastitsio 94–5
    Lasagne 91
    Meatballs 116
    Mince & leek filo pie 46
    Pasta squares with meatballs 86
    Yiayia's roasted stuffed capsicums 160
Portokalopita 197
Potato wedges, Yiayia style 154
potatoes
    Baked fish with onion & potato 105
    Beef, bean & potato stew 112
    Dried red pepper mash 148
    Katina's moussaka 118–19
    Lemon potatoes 145

Meatball soup 65
Okra, tomato & potato casserole 157
Potato wedges, Yiayia style 154
Roasted stuffed vegetables 158
Poure me kokkines piperies 148
Psari kleftiko 102
Psari plaki me kremmidi & patates 105
Psomi spitiko 68
pudding, Rice, with rhubarb 175

R
ragu, Greek-style 131
Red rice with chicken & spinach 82
Revani 186
rhubarb: Rice pudding with rhubarb 175
rice
Baked rice with mince 92
Cabbage rolls 125
Chicken & rice 108
Eftichia's avgolemono 61
Giakoumelos family's avgolemono 62
Meatball soup 65
meatballs 65
Red rice with chicken & spinach 82
Rice pudding with rhubarb 175
Roasted stuffed vegetables 158
Spinach & rice 85
Yiayia's roasted stuffed capsicums 160
Rice pudding with rhubarb 175
ricotta
Filo cheese pie 48–9
Mum's cannelloni 97
Ricotta balls 22
Ricotta balls 22
Rizogalo me raventi 175
Roasted stuffed vegetables 158

S
salad, Garden, Yiayia style 142
sauces
halloumi bechamel 95
traditional bechamel 119
Scrambled eggs with spinach 29
Scrambled eggs, Yiayia style 32
Semolina tray cake 186
Shortbread 'moon' biscuits 172
Sikotakia kotopoulo 113
soups
Bean soup 56
Chicken noodle soup 63
Eftichia's avgolemono 61
Giakoumelos family's avgolemono 62
Lentil soup 58
Meatball soup 65
Spanakopita 38–9
spanakopita dough 38
Spanakorizo 85

spinach
Red rice with chicken & spinach 82
Scrambled eggs with spinach 29
Spanakopita 38–9
Spinach & rice 85
Spinach & rice 85
sterilising jars 89, 146
stews
Beef, bean & potato stew 112
Cabbage & pork stew 115
Strifti pita 42
sugar syrup 186
syrup
lemon syrup 183
lemon–honey syrup 192
orange syrup 197
sugar syrup 186

T
Tiganites piperies me htipita avga 24
Tiganopsomo me feta 73
tips, Pappou's garden 150–1
tips, Yiayia's kitchen 88–9
Tiropita 48–9
Tiropita tis Yiayia 47
tomatoes
Cypriot-style pastitsio 94–5
Fassas family's baked beans 162–3
Garden salad, Yiayia style 142
Greek-style ragu 131
growing tips 151
Katina's moussaka 118–19
Lasagne 91
Mum's cannelloni 97
Okra, tomato & potato casserole 157
Pickled vegetables 146
Roasted stuffed vegetables 158
Spinach & rice 85
traditional bechamel 119
Tsoureki tis Anne 74–5
Tsoureki tis Debbie 78–9

V
Village-style baklava 190
Village-style halva 176

Y
Yemista 158
Yemista tis Yiayia 160
Yiayia's egg & feta filo pie 47
Yiayia's kitchen tips 88–9
Yiayia's roasted stuffed capsicums 160

Z
zucchini: Katina's moussaka 118–19

Pan Macmillan acknowledges the Traditional Custodians of Country throughout Australia and their connections to lands, waters and communities. We pay our respect to Elders past and present and extend that respect to all Aboriginal and Torres Strait Islander peoples today. We honour more than sixty thousand years of storytelling, art and culture.

A Plum book
First published in 2022 by
Pan Macmillan Australia Pty Limited
Level 25, 1 Market Street,
Sydney, NSW 2000, Australia

Level 3, 112 Wellington Parade,
East Melbourne, VIC 3002, Australia

Text copyright © Daniel and Luke Mancuso 2022
Photographs Mark Roper copyright © Pan Macmillan 2022
Design and illustration Daniel New copyright © Pan Macmillan 2022

The moral right of the authors has been asserted.

Book design and illustrations by Daniel New
Yiayia Next Door design by Daniel Mancuso, Now Design
Edited by Lucy Heaver
Index by Helena Holmgren
Photography by Mark Roper
Food and prop styling by Lee Blaylock
Food preparation by Caroline Griffiths, Gemma Smith and Yiayia
Typeset by Hannah Schubert
Colour reproduction by Splitting Image Colour Studio
Printed and bound in China by Imago Printing International Limited

A CIP catalogue record for this book is available from the National Library of Australia.

10 9 8 7 6 5 4 3 2 1